WALKING - - - - - ->
TWIN CITIES

 WILDERNESS PRESS . . . *on the trail since 1967*

WALKING ----➜ TWIN CITIES

35 Tours Exploring Historic Neighborhoods, Lakeside Parks, Gangster Hideouts, Dive Bars, and Cultural Centers of Minneapolis and St. Paul

Third Edition

Holly Day and Sherman Wick

 WILDERNESS PRESS . . . *on the trail since 1967*

Walking Twin Cities: 35 Tours Exploring Historic Neighborhoods, Lakeside Parks, Gangster Hideouts, Dive Bars, and Cultural Centers of Minneapolis and St. Paul

Third edition, first printing
Copyright © 2018 by Holly Day and Sherman Wick
Distributed by Publishers Group West
Manufactured in the United States of America

Cartography and cover design: Scott McGrew; map data: OpenStreetMap
Interior design: Lora Westberg
Project editor: Kate Johnson
Proofreader: Laura Franck
Indexer: Rich Carlson

Cover photo: Stone Arch Bridge in Minneapolis (Hike 13, page 56) by John Eccles/Alamy Stock Photo
Frontispiece: Boats on Lake Calhoun (Hike 2, page 6) by Holly Day and Sherman Wick

Interior photos: Holly Day and Sherman Wick except where noted on page and the following: pages 13 and 43: Richie Diesterheft/Flickr; pages 15 and 17: Dan Downing; page 19: Mark B. Schlemmer/Flickr; page 29: AMB-MD Photography/Shutterstock; page 56: Karen Hermann/Shutterstock; page 62: Jason Riedy/Flickr; page 81: Mark Allan Peterson/Flickr; page 97: Joe Passe/Flickr; page 102: Scott Prokop/Shutterstock; page 105: Quentin Hodges/Flickr; pages 126 and 138: Courtesy of the Minnesota Historical Society; page 128: Joe Ferrer/Shutterstock; pages 142, and 145: David W. Downing; page 151: Scruggelgreen/Shutterstock

Library of Congress Cataloging-in-Publication Data

Names: Day, Holly, author.
Title: Walking Twin Cities : 35 Tours Exploring Historic Neighborhoods, Lakeside Parks, Gangster Hideouts, Dive Bars, and Cultural Centers of Minneapolis and St. Paul / Holly Day and Sherman Wick.
Description: Third Edition. | Birmingham, Alabama : Wilderness Press, an imprint of AdventureKEEN, [2018] | "2nd EDITION 2013"—T.p. verso. | "Distributed by Publishers Group West"—T.p. verso. | Includes index.
Identifiers: LCCN 2018013225| ISBN 9780899978710 (paperback) | ISBN 9780899978727 (ebook)
Subjects: LCSH: Walking—Minnesota—Minneapolis Metropolitan Area—Guidebooks. | Hiking—Minnesota—Minneapolis Metropolitan Area—Guidebooks. | Outdoor recreation—Minnesota—Minneapolis Metropolitan Area—Guidebooks. | Walking—Minnesota—St. Paul Metropolitan Area—Guidebooks. | Hiking—Minnesota—St. Paul Metropolitan Area—Guidebooks. | Outdoor recreation—Minnesota—St. Paul Metropolitan Area—Guidebooks. | Minneapolis Metropolitan Area (Minn.)—Guidebooks. | St. Paul Metropolitan Area (Minn.)—Guidebooks.
Classification: LCC GV199.42.M62 M5634 2018 | DDC 796.5109776/579—dc23
LC record available at lccn.loc.gov/2018013225

Published by  **WILDERNESS PRESS**
An imprint of AdventureKEEN
2204 First Ave. S., Suite 102
Birmingham, AL 35233

Visit wildernesspress.com for a complete listing of our books and for ordering information. Contact us at our website, at facebook.com/wildernesspress1967, or at twitter.com/wilderness1967 with questions or comments. To find out more about who we are and what we're doing, visit blog.wildernesspress.com.

SAFETY NOTICE Although Wilderness Press and the authors have made every attempt to ensure that the information in this book is accurate at press time, they are not responsible for any loss, damage, injury, or inconvenience that may occur to anyone while using this book. You are responsible for your own safety and health while following the walking trips described here.

Dedication

To our grandmothers, Dorothy, Clara, Vera, and Joyce, for their guidance and inspiration

Acknowledgments

With a full year to update the walks, the writing of this edition began, for us, unusually—on a hot summer day. All of the days that came between only reaffirmed our love/hate relationship with Minnesota's unpredictable weather. The biggest difference between writing this edition and the first was having one kid in junior high and one kid grown up and out of the house during most of the writing, as opposed to pushing a toddler in a stroller for most of the walks. Our thanks go to our two children: Wolfgang and Astrid, who are still both the most open people we know about visiting new places and trying new things. A big thank-you goes to our agent, Matt Wagner, and all the people at Wilderness Press for making this book possible.

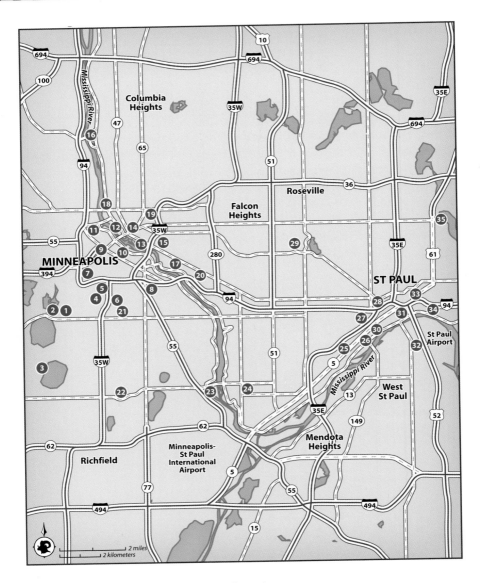

Numbers on this locator map correspond to walk numbers.

Table of Contents

Acknowledgments v

Overview Map vi

Authors' Note ix

Introduction 1

1 Uptown 2

2 Lake Calhoun/Bde Maka Ska 6

3 Lake Harriet 10

4 Nicollet Avenue's Eat Street 15

5 Whittier 23

6 Phillips and Elliot Park 23

7 Loring Park and the Walker Art Center 29

8 Cedar-Riverside 34

9 Minneapolis Downtown and Theater District 39

10 Downtown/Washington Avenue 43

11 Warehouse District/North Loop 47

12 Bridge Square, the Gateway, Boom Island, Nicollet Island,
and the North Loop 51

13 Historic Mill District 56

14 East Hennepin/Marcy-Holmes 62

15 Dinkytown 66

16 North Mississippi Regional Park and Webber Park 70

17 U of M 73

18 Nordeast Minneapolis 78

19 Northeast Breweries Tour and Central Avenue Business District 84

20 Prospect Park's Tower Hill Park and Water Tower 88

21 Minneapolis's Lake Street 92

22 Minnehaha Parkway/48th and Chicago 97

23 Minnehaha Falls 102

24 Highland Park and Hidden Falls Regional Park 107

25 West Seventh Street 112

26 High Bridge and Cherokee Regional Park 116

27 Cathedral, Ramsey, and Summit Hills 120

28 Minnesota State Capitol 126

29 Como Park 131

30 Irvine Park and West Seventh Street 136

31 Downtown St. Paul 142

32 West Side 147

33 Swede Hollow/Dayton's Bluff 151

34 Indian Mounds Regional Park/Bruce Vento Nature Sanctuary 155

35 Payne-Phalen 160

Appendix: Walks by Theme **164**

Index **166**

About the Authors **174**

Authors' Note

Minnesotans love to talk about the weather—spend any time here, and you'll understand why. A sunny summertime morning can easily turn into a rainy afternoon, and snow can surprise you as late as early May. A good rule of thumb is to check the forecast before heading out, and to make sure that you dress sensibly according to the time of year. Another thing to keep in mind is that as cities evolve, landmarks change. We've tried to mention only landmarks that we're sure will stand the test of time, but you never can account for bad city planning or gentrification.

When navigating Minneapolis, it's especially important to pay attention to the street signs indicating Street, Avenue, North, South, Northeast, Southeast, and so on. The city is laid out in a nice, neat grid, but newcomers not used to streets bearing multiple names can get easily lost. St. Paul is a little trickier, due to its poorly plotted street design adapted to a much more difficult, hilly topography. This is why we recommend that visitors and residents alike use the map in the *Hudson's Twin Cities Street Atlas;* we have included *Hudson's* coordinates for all of the walks in this book.

One new addition to getting around the Twin Cities is the expansion into St. Paul of the Nice Ride bike system, which allows visitors to rent bicycles to get from one place to another for a nominal fee without having to resort to driving or taking the bus. This system is a large part of the reason why Minneapolis has been named America's Best Bike City by *Bicycling* magazine. For more information about where to find and check out Nice Ride Bikes, see niceridemn.org. They've recently expanded rental transportation options along the Minneapolis riverfront with kayak and canoe rentals from Mississippi River Paddle Share (paddleshare.org). Future plans include expansion into St. Paul.

We hope that this book inspires you to investigate the great possibilities the Twin Cities offer. Once again, happy trails!

North Mississippi Regional Park (Walk 16, page 70)

Introduction

Even though they're often lumped together, the Twin Cities are two distinct cities with very different histories. Minneapolis is the Mill City, the City of Lakes, composed mostly of flat prairies. St. Paul is the Capital City, built on rolling hills and high river bluffs.

Culturally, the cities have their differences, too. Minneapolis is home to world-renowned theaters and modern art galleries, while St. Paul is the home of many of the state's institutions, from the seat of government to the seat of the Roman Catholic Archdiocese of St. Paul and Minneapolis. Minneapolis is a newer city, which is reflected in the architecture and overall vibe, while St. Paul's older neighborhoods feature some of the most intact Victorian-era houses in the country. Because of their locations on the west and east sides of the Mississippi River, it is said that Minneapolis is more like a modern West Coast city, while St. Paul is akin to a historic East Coast city.

The two are linked by the Mississippi River—the same force that shaped their origins. St. Paul developed earlier, mostly because it was more easily accessible via the river. Thanks to the foresight of the civic-conscious Victorians who succeeded the cities' founders, both cities set aside large tracts of land for public use all along the rivers and lakes. Some of the most beautiful parks were plotted in the early days of the cities.

Even today there are big differences between the cities. For example, St. Paulites, gluttons for punishment, host the annual Winter Carnival during the coldest time of the year. Minneapolitans take the easy way out by celebrating the Aquatennial Festival each summer. Despite having their city festivals at opposite ends of the solstice, Minnesotans love the outdoors. Even with the notoriously fierce winters, they statistically spend more time outside than most.

With this edition, for the first time since the 1920s, both cities' populations have grown in relation to the Twin Cities region, by 37,000 in Minneapolis and 19,000 in St. Paul. Such tremendous growth, in the wake of pent-up demand after the Great Recession, has led to increased rents and property values, while available amenities—restaurants, clubs, bars, parks, and transportation infrastructure—have sprung up in vacant lots, former rail yards, abandoned industrial buildings, and parking lots. This growth is reflected in this edition's additional walks, walks featuring former industrial ruins converted into taprooms, restaurants, and other businesses, run by a community of genuine artisans, with the Surly Bill (2011) as a major impetus.

Whether you're interested in art, culture, history, or nature, there's a walk in this book designed for you. We hope that it serves not only as a guidebook for (re)discovering the Twin Cities but also as a springboard for additional explorations.

1 Uptown
Cool Place for Fun in the Hot Summer Sun

Above: *Stella's Fish Café*

BOUNDARIES: 31st St. W., Irving Ave. S., 26th St. W., Fremont Ave. S.
HUDSON'S TWIN CITIES STREET ATLAS COORDINATES: Map 394, 1D
DISTANCE: About 1.5 miles
DIFFICULTY: Easy
PARKING: Free parking on The Mall
PUBLIC TRANSIT: Numerous bus lines to Uptown Station (located at Hennepin Ave. S. and the end of The Mall)

Uptown is the Twin Cities' place for fun—especially during summertime. It's not officially recognized as a neighborhood by the City of Minneapolis, and it's actually composed of sections of the Calhoun, East Calhoun, East Isles, and Lowry East neighborhoods. It became a de facto second downtown after Calhoun Square opened in 1983, combining extant buildings and new construction to create an urban shopping center. With its almost endless array of entertainment options—including bars, coffee shops, restaurants, music clubs, comedy clubs, movie theaters, art galleries, shopping, and tattoo parlors—the area attracts hip, young crowds. In recent years, these crowds have increased with the proliferation of multistory apartments and condos along the Midtown Greenway. The proximity to Lake Calhoun and Lake of the Isles only heightens the cachet of the area during warm weather, when, after a day at the beach, locals enjoy the neighborhood amenities. Put all these together and it makes for a fun and often playfully raucous neighborhood—and a great place for a walk.

Walk Description

Begin at the west corner of Uptown Station (bus stop) and turn left, heading north on Hennepin Avenue South. As you follow the gradual slope downhill, notice the funky grandeur of this stretch of Uptown, an often incongruent combination of architectural styles where beautifully restored storefronts sit uneasily beside cookie-cutter strip mall buildings. In recent years, more national chain businesses have appeared. At the corner of 28th Street West at Allina Health is the original inscribed lintel for West High School, defunct since 1982.

Turn right on 26th Street West and immediately turn right again, going south on Hennepin Avenue South. Continue south on Hennepin as the avenue cuts through the grid at Girard Avenue South, passing the Mount Royal Apartments. On the left is ❶ **Saint Sabrina's,** the professional tattooing and ear- and body-piercing parlor. After opening in 1993, the parlor moved to the new location in 2006 and slightly de-emphasized the purgatory and hell themes. Free coffee, tea, and movies are offered to customers in a comfortable and relaxed atmosphere.

Cross 28th Street West. On the left, as you continue on the east side of the street, the ❷ **Tibet Store** sells the best from the spiritual homeland of the Dalai Lama. The store stocks reasonably priced clothing, as well as jewelry and Tibetan Buddhist books. Just ahead down the hill is the ❸ **Williams Uptown Pub & Peanut Bar.** This popular hangout serves 300 bottled brews and 70 draft beers with good bar food upstairs. Free popcorn, peanuts, games, and darts are available in the basement. Kitty-corner on Lagoon Avenue is the marquee of Landmark Theatres' recently renovated moderne-style ❹ **Uptown Theatre,** a gateway to the business district since 1939.

Turn left on Lagoon Avenue. At the corner of Girard Avenue South is the Uptown's sister theater—Landmark's ❺ **Lagoon Cinema,** with five screens specializing in art house, indie, and foreign films. Turn right on Fremont Avenue South. To the left is the oddball color scheme of the New Traditional–style Uptown City Apartments.

Turn right on Lake Street West and cross Girard Avenue South to get to ❻ **Stella's Fish Café & Prestige Oyster Bar.** There you'll get fresh seafood and plenty of alcohol in this lovely renovated restaurant with rooftop dining and lots of hip, young things in the summer.

Uptown Art Fair: Art and Sun

Uptown is the summer-fun place for the Twin Cities, and the annual Uptown Art Fair is the pinnacle of seasonal merriment. Locals and visitors from around the world enjoy one of the Midwest's premier fine-art festivals, usually scheduled for the first weekend in August—one of the few times when warm weather is almost guaranteed. With 450 artists juried and evaluated by professionals, the quality of the art is as excellent as it is diverse and includes something for almost anyone. There are incredible people-watching opportunities as more than 300,000 visitors descend for the three-day weekend event. The first Uptown Art Fair was held in 1963, and it attracted a small yet enthusiastic crowd. Over time, the event grew—too large by the early 1990s, when more than 600 exhibitors displayed their wares; since then it has become more selective and competitive. It remains a favorite event for those browsing for art or simply enjoying summer in the Twin Cities.

Turn left on Hennepin Avenue South where ❼ **Calhoun Square** is located. ❽ **Roat Osha** offers excellent, authentic, and locally inspired Thai food in a happy hour–friendly atmosphere. Uptown became an essential shopping destination after this retail center opened. Unfortunately, in recent years business has waned, and it has gone through a succession of ownership groups that have tried to reinvent the center.

Turn right on 31st Street West and right again on Hennepin Avenue South. Just past the stunning and unusual Spanish Churrigueresque Revival façade of the now-closed Suburban World Theatre (1927) is the former site of the Uptown Bar and Café, once a popular performance space for local and national bands and now a big-box store.

Turn left on Lake Street West. after passing a half block of national chains. On the right is ❾ **Mesa Pizza Uptown,** a satellite of the popular pizza place in Dinkytown, selling cheap pizza by the slice until the late-night hours.

Turn right on Irving Avenue South. On the northwest corner of Lake Street is ❿ **Barbette**—fine dining for cool folks.

Turn right on Lagoon Avenue.

Turn left on Hennepin Avenue South and finish the walk at Uptown Station.

Points of Interest

1. **Saint Sabrina's** saintsabrinas.com, 2645 Hennepin Ave. S., Minneapolis, 612-874-7360

2. **Tibet Store** tibetstorempls.com, 2835 Hennepin Ave. S., Minneapolis, 612-872-8800

3. **Williams Uptown Pub & Peanut Bar** williamsminneapolis.com, 2911 Hennepin Ave. S., Minneapolis, 612-823-6271

4. **Uptown Theatre** landmarktheatres.com, 2906 Hennepin Ave. S., Minneapolis, 612-825-6006

5. **Lagoon Cinema** landmarktheatres.com, 1320 Lagoon Ave., Minneapolis, 612-825-6006

6. **Stella's Fish Café & Prestige Oyster Bar** stellasfishcafe.com, 1400 Lake St. W., Minneapolis, 612-824-8862

7. **Calhoun Square** calhounsquare.com, 3001 Hennepin Ave. S., Minneapolis, 612-824-1240

8. **Roat Osha** roatoshathai.com, 3001 Hennepin Ave., Ste. 1370, Minneapolis, 612-377-4418

9. **Mesa Pizza Uptown** mesapizzamn.com/Uptown, 1440 Lake St. W., Minneapolis, 612-206-3206

10. **Barbette** barbette.com, 1600 Lake St. W., Minneapolis, 612-827-5710

2 Lake Calhoun/Bde Maka Ska
Biggest Pearl in the Chain of Lakes

Above: *Summer day on Lake Calhoun*

BOUNDARIES: Lake St. W., Zenith Ave. S., Calhoun Pkwy. W., Calhoun Pkwy. E., Irving Ave. S.
HUDSON'S TWIN CITIES STREET ATLAS COORDINATES: Map 393, 5D; Map 420, 5A; Map 394, 1D
DISTANCE: About 3.25 miles
DIFFICULTY: Easy but long
PARKING: Free parking on The Mall, located at Mall and Knox Ave. S.
PUBLIC TRANSIT: Bus lines 4, 6, and 23

Lake Calhoun/Bde Maka Ska is the largest lake in Minneapolis's popular Chain of Lakes system, which includes Lake Harriet, Brownie Lake, Lake of the Isles, and Cedar Lake. Bde Maka Ska, the Dakota name for the Lake, has been recently restored by the Park Board, with plans in the future to commemorate the history of Cloud Man's Village. It is also a part of the Grand Rounds Scenic Byway, a 50-mile route that connects many of Minneapolis's parks and lakes. Theoretically, with only a few tiny gaps in the circuit, you can travel from park to park by foot or bicycle via the Grand

Rounds without ever having to get in a car. All around Lake Calhoun are sandy, well-maintained beaches, perfect for swimming or sunbathing—or, if you'd prefer, you can take a break from walking and rent a canoe or paddleboat instead.

Walk Description

Start across the street from the corner of Mall and Knox Avenue South. Go straight, briefly heading west before the path curves south, toward the water and to your left.

Take your first left to walk along Lake Calhoun. Off to your right is the path leading to Lake of the Isles, which is another great bird-watching and hiking area.

At the fork, keep right to continue following the lake on the walking path. To your left is a little marsh where you might see baby wood ducks and mallards in late spring and early summer, while to the right is the full arc of the lake. During hot and dry summers, the water level can get low enough that the waterway becomes choked with duckweed and water lilies; when the season is wet and rainy, many of these paths become completely submerged.

Go under the Lake Street Bridge and keep going straight. Follow the path up the hill.

At the canoe rental and boat launch, turn left just before the boat launch and go up the hill toward the street.

Turn left to follow Lake Street West to go over the bridge that you just walked under. Stay on the left side of the path marked with the pedestrian sign or you might get clobbered by a cyclist.

Follow the pedestrian path down the hill and continue on the path to follow the lakeshore. All summer long, this is the place to watch sailboats and other human- and wind-powered crafts on the lake. In the wintertime, a few hardy individuals head out onto the frozen surface of the lake to go ice sailing, which is a lot like windsurfing.

Follow the curve of the lake until the shoreline gets sandy. You can leave the concrete path to walk along the beach; both paths lead in the same direction. The sandy path opens up into ❶ Lake Calhoun North Beach, a popular swimming beach complete with lifeguard. If you brought a towel along, this is a great place for a dip—or just roll up your pants for a knee-deep wade.

Follow the path past the beach and keep going straight. To the right is a playground, a great diversion if you have kids with you. Keep straight to follow the lakeshore. To the left, the sandy shore turns into boulders installed by the city to protect the shoreline from further erosion.

Keep following the shoreline. After a while, the right side of the street becomes lined with tree-covered bluffs, and for the next couple of blocks every house on your right is a grand mansion—new or old. At the end of the block are the sprawling grounds of ❷ The Bakken: A Library and Museum of Electricity in Life. The gigantic stone fortress was originally designed by entrepreneur William Goodfellow in the 1930s to impress a woman who called him cheap. The museum has an amazing collection of antique electrical instruments used for musical and scientific purposes. You can easily access the Bakken from here—the first fork in the path (at 36th Street West) heads off to the right toward the museum.

Go straight past the fork to continue along the lakeshore. To your right is a large picnic area, with tables and a sand volleyball court. In the summer, these grounds are packed with parkgoers enjoying the warm sun and cool breezes coming off the water.

Go straight at the next fork to continue following the lakeshore. Just past the parking lot is ❸ **Thomas Beach,** another popular swimming beach.

Cross the path driveway to continue. At the side of the path is a pump-operated drinking fountain with a dog bowl, from which four-legged hikers can drink.

From here, you get a great view of downtown Minneapolis on the far side of the lake, and to the side of the downtown skyline you can see the distinctive dome of St. Mary's Greek Orthodox Church. Up ahead and to your left, you'll see a little wooden dock. If you like to fish, come early, or be prepared to share the dock with other avid fishermen. To your right, just past the fishing dock, is the Lake Calhoun archery range, and just past it is historic ❹ **Lakewood Memorial Cemetery.** The 125-year-old cemetery is absolutely huge; it's open to the public seven days a week, year-round.

Keep following the path. On your right, keep an eye out for the boulder that marks the first dwelling in what would become Minneapolis. This marker commemorates the spot where Samuel W. and Gideon Pond, who came to Minnesota to convert American Indians to Christianity, built their mission in 1834. The gold-domed ❺ **St. Mary's Greek Orthodox Church** up the hill at 3450 Irving Avenue South was built virtually on top of the Ponds' original mission in 1957.

Keep going straight. Up the first set of stairs and to the right is the ❻ **Minnesota Zen Meditation Center.** Open to the public, it offers classes on meditation as well as quiet garden spots perfect for individual practice. About a block north, you'll find Lake Calhoun's newest swimming beach, the ❼ **32nd Street Beach.**

Continue north, following the curve of the lake, until you reach the red-roofed white park pavilion, where plenty of picnic tables look out over the lake. You can also rent a canoe or paddleboat or go for a gondola ride from the pavilion.

From the pavilion, go straight past the canoe/paddleboat rentals and take the walking path to follow the shoreline.

Go straight (north) on the pedestrian path and under the Lake Street Bridge.

Follow the path past the marshland and take your first right.

Go straight to the street crossing of Mall and Knox Avenue, and you're back where you started.

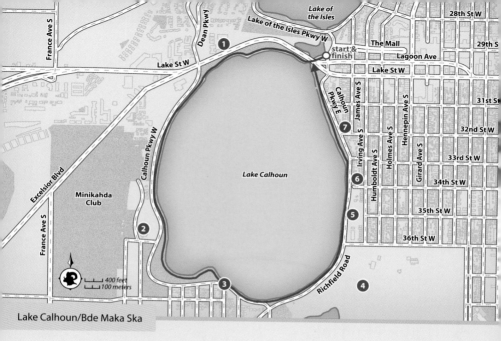

Lake Calhoun/Bde Maka Ska

Points of Interest

1 **Lake Calhoun North Beach** minneapolisparks.org, 2710 Lake St. W., Minneapolis, MN 55417, 612-230-6400

2 **The Bakken: A Library and Museum of Electricity in Life** thebakken.org, 3537 Zenith Ave. S., Minneapolis, 612-926-3878

3 **Thomas Beach** minneapolisparks.org, Thomas Ave. S and Calhoun Pkwy. W., Minneapolis, 612-230-6400

4 **Lakewood Memorial Cemetery** lakewoodcemetery.com, 3600 Hennepin Ave., Minneapolis, 612-822-2171

5 **St. Mary's Greek Orthodox Church** stmarysgoc.org, 3450 Irving Ave. S., Minneapolis, 612-825-2247

6 **Minnesota Zen Meditation Center** mnzencenter.org, 3343 Calhoun Pkwy. E., Minneapolis, 612-822-5313

7 **32nd Street Beach** minneapolisparks.org, 3200 Calhoun Pkwy. E., Minneapolis, 612-230-6400

3 Lake Harriet
Wildlife in the Heart of the City

Above: Lake Harriet Pavilion

BOUNDARIES: 50th St. W., W. Lake Harriet Pkwy., William Berry Dr., Kings Hwy., E. Lake Harriet Pkwy.
HUDSON'S TWIN CITIES STREET ATLAS COORDINATES: Map 420, 5A and 5B; Map 421, 1A and 1B
DISTANCE: About 3.5 miles
DIFFICULTY: Moderate
PARKING: Free parking on Lake Harriet Pkwy. and nearby side streets
PUBLIC TRANSIT: Bus lines 4, 6, and 23

You may have noticed that a few sites in the Twin Cities bear the name Harriet. As a general rule, the Harriet sites in St. Paul are named after Harriet Bishop, who was the first schoolteacher in St. Paul, while the Harriet sites in Minneapolis are named after Harriet Lovejoy, the wife of Colonel Henry Leavenworth. According to legend, Leavenworth missed his wife very much while he was stationed at Fort Snelling, so he named just about anything beautiful he came across after her.

Today, Lake Harriet is still one of the loveliest lakes in the region, attracting throngs of park-goers year-round. Along the banks of the lake are hiking and biking trails, benches for bird-watching, places to eat, and, of course, the historic Lake Harriet Bandshell, which features live music during the summertime. Nearby are the Lyndale Park Rose Gardens, historic Memorial Cemetery, Lyndale Park Peace Garden, Como–Harriet Streetcar Line, and Roberts Bird Sanctuary.

Walk Description

Start at the LAKE HARRIET park sign, just south of the corner of 42nd Street West and West Lake Harriet Parkway. Facing the lake, make a right to walk along the lakeshore. In early spring you'll see flocks of loons migrating north; mallards, seagulls, wood ducks, and Canada geese are present all spring and summer. All along the lake numerous benches face the water, so if you want to stop and simply take in everything, there are lots of comfortable places to sit. To your right is the Twin Cities historic streetcar line. If you enjoy fishing, try out one of the many spots for shore fishing along the banks. The first set of steps you pass leads up to ❶ **Beard's Plaisance Park,** with public tennis courts, a picnic area, and a hilltop pavilion that can be reserved for special occasions.

Keep following the path around the lake. Just past the long fishing pier to your left, you'll pass a group of marshy islands and a little scenic overlook. This is a great spot to see ducks and geese as well as their offspring.

Cross the little wooden bridge and keep following the curve of the shoreline. You can see the scope of the Lake Harriet Bandshell and, in the summer, dozens of sailboats across the lake from here.

Take the first tall set of steps to your right and go all the way to the top to Queen Avenue South and Lake Harriet Parkway.

Cross the street and turn left to follow Lake Harriet Parkway.

At Penn Avenue South, turn right. This takes you through the modern, upscale Lynnhurst neighborhood, where McMansions are constantly springing up.

Cross 49th Street West and keep going straight. At the bottom of the hill is a little neighborhood business district, with the excellent Italian restaurants ❷ **Broders' Pasta Bar** and ❸ **Broders' Cucina Italiana.** Broders' Pasta Bar is an intimate and elegant Italian restaurant that opens only for dinner, with items such as crab lasagna and stuffed mussels on its menu. Across the street, the Cucina carries the same quality of food but serves it in a more relaxed, café-style setting. ❹ **Terzo**—a wine bar with a porchetteria window and beautiful outside patio—is the newest of the Broders'-run restaurants.

Turn left at 50th Street West. Turn left at Oliver Ave South, heading north.

Cross the street at Lake Harriet Parkway and take the steps all the way down to the walking path below. You can see the Lake Harriet Pavilion and the downtown Minneapolis skyline far across on the other side of the lake.

Turn right to follow the walking path around the lake. To your right are some of the most magnificent mansions along this walk.

At the green water pump is ❺ **Lake Harriet Southeast Beach,** a small swimming beach.

Continue on the path around the lake. When you pass the boat racks on your left, take the right fork and cross East Lake Harriet Parkway. Make an immediate right to cross Roseway Road.

Cut through the grass down the hill to get to the little path at the bottom. Take the path through the gate and go straight.

You're now inside the ❻ **Lyndale Park Rose Garden,** the second-oldest public rose garden in the United States. The garden was designed by Theodore Wirth, who also designed the country's oldest public rose garden, in Connecticut, and who served as parks superintendent for Minneapolis from 1906 to 1938 and designed most of the city's fabulous parks.

Head north through the rose garden and around the Italian Heffelfinger Fountain. Turn left to walk alongside the Lyndale Park Perennial and Annual Display Garden, built in 1963 when the Phelps Fountain (the one with the turtles, located straight ahead) was moved here from Gateway Park in downtown Minneapolis. The garden contains hundreds of exotic and native plants, all clearly identified.

Follow the gravel path to the right, and turn left at the sidewalk to cross Roseway Road. To your right is the Lyndale Park Peace (Rock) Garden, containing a wide variety of pine trees from all over the world, as well as willows, grasses, and thousands of flower varieties.

Follow the sidewalk to the parking lot. Go straight to pass through the little wooden structure and enter the Thomas Sadler Roberts Bird Sanctuary, named after the notable ornithologist whose 1919 book, *A Review of the Ornithology of Minnesota,* is still one of the best-selling Minnesota-themed bird books of all time.

Turn right to go onto the plank pathway and follow it through the sanctuary. While you might not be able to see many birds inside, you'll certainly hear hundreds of them all around you.

Take a left at the end of the plastic boardwalk. To your left are dense reed- and cattail-filled wetlands, home to orioles, red-winged blackbirds, and other songbirds; to your right is a swampy marsh where you can usually spot waterfowl families.

Go straight to the second plastic boardwalk and turn right. This takes you directly through the marsh, where you can get a closer look at some of the waterbirds that live here. Be careful

The Linden Hills station of the Como–Harriet Streetcar Line

through the last part of the boardwalk, as flooding sometimes causes it to dip underwater as you're walking over it.

Turn left at the end of the boardwalk. To your left is another waterfowl nesting site, as well as the back end of ➐ **Lakewood Memorial Cemetery.** The fallen trees in the dense forest nearby have been intentionally left to naturally compost. In the hot, sweaty days of late summer, you can see spectacular bright orange and yellow bracket mushrooms on many of the dead logs.

Go straight past the fork to follow the Lakewood Memorial Cemetery fence. Go through the gate and up the stairs to the street.

Cross the street to the parking lot. Continue west, straight through the lot, and cut across the bicycle path (watch for zooming bicyclists) until you get to the pedestrian path.

Turn left slightly on the path. This takes you by the ➑ **Lake Harriet Band Shell,** officially the fifth music pavilion to be built on this site since the original was erected in 1888. The restrooms to your right were built in 1891 but fortunately feature completely modern facilities inside. Picnic tables are up the hill from here to your right.

Follow the sidewalk toward the lake. The smaller building by the band shell has more restrooms inside, as well as ➒ **Bread & Pickle,** where you can buy seafood, beer, hot dogs, burgers, and ice cream. There's no indoor dining, but many picnic tables nearby look out onto the water.

Follow the path to the right and go straight. Up to the right at the top of the hill is the station for the ➓ **Como–Harriet Streetcar Line,** which takes passengers down the last remaining original tracks of the famed Twin Cities streetcar line to Lakewood Memorial Cemetery and back. (Note that the streetcar line operates only May–October on select days; check the website for its schedule.) Straight ahead of you is the LAKE HARRIET sign, the starting point.

Points of Interest

1. **Beard's Plaisance Park** minneapolisparks.org, 45th St. W. and Upton Ave. S., Minneapolis, 612-230-6400

2. **Broders' Pasta Bar** broderspastabar.com, 5000 Penn Ave. S., Minneapolis, 612-925-9202

3. **Broders' Cucina Italiana** broders.com, 2308 50th St. W., Minneapolis, 612-925-3113

4. **Terzo** terzompls.com, 2221 50th Street W., Minneapolis, 612-925-0330

5. **Lake Harriet Southeast Beach** minneapolisparks.org, 4740 Lake Harriet Pkwy. E., Minneapolis, 612-230-6400

6. **Lyndale Park Rose Garden** minneapolisparks.org, 4124 Roseway Rd., Minneapolis, 612-230-6400

7. **Lakewood Memorial Cemetery** lakewoodcemetery.com, 3600 Hennepin Ave., Minneapolis, 612-822-2171

8. **Lake Harriet Band Shell** minneapolisparks.org, 4135 W. Lake Harriet Pkwy., Minneapolis, 612-230-6400

9. **Bread & Pickle** breadandpickle.com, 4135 Lake Harriet Pkwy. W., Minneapolis, 612-767-9009

10. **Como–Harriet Streetcar Line** trolleyride.org, 2330 42nd St. W., Minneapolis, 651-228-0263

4 Nicollet Avenue's Eat Street
Where the Twin Cities Eat Global Locally

Above: *Spyhouse Espresso Bar & Gallery*

BOUNDARIES: 29th St. W., Nicollet Ave., Grant St. W.
HUDSON'S TWIN CITIES STREET ATLAS COORDINATES: Map 394, 2C and 2D
DISTANCE: About. 2.75 miles
DIFFICULTY: Easy
PARKING: Free parking on 25th St.; free parking (2 hours or less) on Nicollet Ave.
PUBLIC TRANSIT: Bus lines 2, 4, 113, and 115

Eat Street is Minneapolis's culinary connection to the world, boasting 17 city blocks of restaurants, markets, and coffee shops with food from around the world. It's a destination for both novices and experienced foodies in search of toothsome adventures. Nicollet Avenue cuts through three neighborhoods—most prominently Whittier, once an affluent area that fell into dilapidation in the 1970s in the wake of the wealthy moving to the suburbs and the construction of I-35W. Immigrants from mostly Asia—and later the Middle East, Europe, Mexico, and Africa—converted a wide array of buildings into restaurants. Over time it has become the incredible all-American ethnic food area known as Eat Street.

Bring a hearty appetite with you for this walk, which follows Nicollet Avenue to the outskirts of downtown Minneapolis and Loring Park, through Stevens Square, and back to Whittier. At last count, more than 55 businesses for dine-in or takeout food from around the world were located in this ever-changing whirlwind of a neighborhood. The area is always in transition, with new Americans taking language classes and participating in start-up businesses on the same street, while new condos and chains keep moving in. Its culinary impact has expanded to abutting streets—26th Street and Nicollet Avenue and south of Lake Street also have large-scale food scenes. Take a walk and see Minneapolis's gateway to world cuisine in the scenic shadows of downtown.

Walk Description

Start at the corner of 25th Street West and Nicollet Avenue in front of hipster and artist hangout ❶ **Spyhouse Espresso Bar and Gallery.** Cross 25th Street and head north up Nicollet Avenue.

Keep straight, crossing 24th Street West. The next few blocks are home to several schools that teach English as a second language for both children and adults, including the English Language Immersion School and the Somali Education Center. Up ahead are non-food-related ethnic businesses such as hair salons and financial planners, as well as apartments and recent cookie-cutter condo developments with national-chain franchises at street level.

After you cross Franklin, Eat Street enters the Loring Park neighborhood. Cross 18th Street West and go straight. From here, you can see the perpetual transition that is Eat Street, where vacant lots sit beside both fledgling and well-established businesses, all close to the downtown skyline. Since the beginning of the new millennium, condos have become increasingly common.

Turn left at Grant Street West, and then immediately turn left again to follow Nicollet Avenue past a block of condos. The next block has high-quality restaurants.

Cross 18th Street West and you'll come to the ❷ **Plymouth Congregational Church** (1908), a Gothic Revival church made of granite and limestone. Just past Franklin Avenue on the right is the Art Deco sign of Franklin-Nicollet Liquor, especially cool-looking when illuminated in the evening.

Cross 25th Street West, passing an exciting assortment of restaurants and ethnic grocery stores, as well as the innovative nightclub and restaurant ❸ **Icehouse.**

Cross 26th Street West. ❹ **Peninsula Malaysian Cuisine** offers delicious authentic food from a nation where Chinese, Malaysian, and Indian food traditions have combined for centuries to create outstanding polyglot dishes such as roti *canai,* fish in banana leaf, and beef *rendang.* Continue

Icehouse offers American cuisine, an extensive selection of drinks, and live music in an industrial setting.

straight, crossing 29th Street West. Near the end of the street is access to the Midtown Greenway, a pedestrian/bicycle path connecting Uptown and the lakes to West River Parkway.

Turn left at the end of the street and then left again, returning to Nicollet Avenue. ⑤ **Pho Tau Bay** serves, as the sign says, "the best soup in town," and includes a full Vietnamese menu that even the parsimonious can afford.

Continue straight, crossing 28th Street West. On the right is ⑥ **Rainbow Chinese Restaurant and Bar.** Since 1987, chef and owner Tammy Wong has provided fresh and inventive fine Chinese food. On the next block is local favorite ⑦ **Quang,** which features tasty Vietnamese cuisine. The next local favorite is the ⑧ **Black Forest Inn,** which for more than 50 years has served excellent German food, including sauerbraten, schnitzel, and bratwurst. In the summertime, you can dine outside in the beautifully designed Beer Garden, a charming natural oasis secluded on the busy street by trees, shrubs, flowers, and a fountain.

Cross 26th Street West. Up the block at 2539 Nicollet Avenue is ⑨ **Pancho Villa,** specializing in outstanding seafood and authentic Mexican food. The building was the longtime home of Twin/Tone Records, the label for local indie stalwarts such as The Replacements and Soul Asylum. The address, then 2541, became the title of a great song on the late Grant Hart's first post–Hüsker Dü solo album, *Intolerance*. Continue to the corner of 25th Street West to finish the walk.

Nicollet Avenue's Eat Street

Points of Interest

1. **Spyhouse Espresso Bar and Gallery** spyhousecoffee.com, 2451 Nicollet Ave., Minneapolis, 612-871-3177

2. **Plymouth Congregational Church** plymouth.org, 1900 Nicollet Ave., Minneapolis, 612-871-7400

3. **Icehouse** icehousempls.com, 2528 Nicollet Ave., Minneapolis, 612-276-6523

4. **Peninsula Malaysian Cuisine** peninsulamalaysiancuisine.com, 2608 Nicollet Ave., Minneapolis, 612-871-8282

5. **Pho Tau Bay** photaubay.us, 2837 Nicollet Ave., Minneapolis, 612-874-6030

6. **Rainbow Chinese Restaurant and Bar** rainbowrestaurant.com, 2739 Nicollet Ave., Minneapolis, 612-870-7081

7. **Quang** quang-restaurant.com, 2719 Nicollet Ave., Minneapolis, 612-874-6030

8. **Black Forest Inn** blackforestinnmpls.com, 1 26th St. E., Minneapolis, 612-872-0812

9. **Pancho Villa Mexican Restaurant** panchovillasgrill.com, 2539 Nicollet Ave., Minneapolis, 612-871-7014

5 Whittier

Mia and Washburn Fair Oaks: Art and Nature Come Alive

Above: Minneapolis Institute of Art (Mia)

BOUNDARIES: 26th St. E., First Ave. S., Franklin Ave. E., Third Ave. S.
HUDSON'S TWIN CITIES STREET ATLAS COORDINATES: Map 394, 2C and 2D
DISTANCE: About 1.5 miles
DIFFICULTY: Easy
PARKING: Free parking on 22nd St. E.
PUBLIC TRANSIT: Bus lines 2, 5, 17, and 580

The Whittier neighborhood walk connects the past with the present via the principal source of wealth in Minneapolis's early days: flour. The mansions, Washburn Fair Oaks Park, and even the Minneapolis Institute of Art (Mia) are all beneficiaries of the affluence created by the Mill Cities' founders. They moved here, far south of downtown, to escape the grimy and filthy Mississippi River. Early in the 20th century, the urban blight they left behind had caught up with them—and the majority of the wealthy moved farther from the city's core. No longer strictly a bastion of the well-to-do, Whittier is home to a diverse group of immigrants, working-class and middle-class residents, young people, artists, and, of course, those living in historic mansions.

Walk Description

Begin on the southwest corner of 22nd Street East and go south on Third Avenue South. On the right is ❶ **Washburn Fair Oaks Park,** until 1924 the site of William Washburn's enormous stone mansion. After making his fortune in the flour-milling industry at St. Anthony Falls, he was elected to the U.S. House of Representatives and later to the U.S. Senate. On the left is the Gothic and Renaissance–inspired ❷ **Hennepin History Museum.** Originally the George H. and Leonora Christian House (George was an early manager of the Washburn Crosby Company, which later became General Mills), it's now the home of the Hennepin County History Society.

Continue straight, crossing 24th Street East. On the right is the rather prosaic modernist 1974 addition to the ❸ **Minneapolis Institute of Art.** Connected to the entrance is the ❹ **Children's Theatre Company,** expanded with a kid-friendly design by architect Michael Graves in 2005. Across the street are fine examples of the Colonial Revival style, the Fair Oaks Apartments (1940). Courtyards and lush gardens complement the one- and two-bedroom units.

After passing the Children's Theatre, continue on Third Avenue South. The 2500 block was the location of the Dorilus Morrison House (1858), home to the first mayor of Minneapolis. The building was razed to make room for the south portion of Mia in 1915.

Turn right on 26th Street. This section of Whittier is a modest residential area for hipsters. Continuing on 26th, you'll see the back of ❺ **Minneapolis College of Art and Design** (MCAD). Since 1974 it has provided an excellent fine-arts education and now has more than 700 students.

Turn right on Stevens Avenue South. To the right is MCAD's main entrance, complete with sculptures. Across the street are fine examples of quirkily renovated Victorian homes, with superbly unusual color combinations. Up ahead and on the right is the 2006 addition by Michael Graves, the aforementioned architect and Target product designer. The addition dovetails with the existing Mia structure, and the added gallery space is especially welcome.

Continue on Stevens Avenue South. At 24th Street East is Washburn Fair Oaks Park.

Cross 22nd Street East, where you can view the Beaux Arts perfection known as the Gale Mansion (1912) on the corner (at 2115 Stevens Ave. S.). With its lovely Renaissance Revival–inspired features, it stands out as an architectural gem.

Turn left on 22nd Street East for a closer look at the mansions that define the area, such as the Alfred F. Pillsbury House (116 22nd St. E.), a huge Tudor Revival constructed with local limestone. Alfred was the son of John Pillsbury, who founded the world-famous food company. The next

Mia: Art Through the Ages Without the Price of Admission

The Minneapolis Institute of Art, rebranded as "Mia," has a staggering art collection in terms of depth and especially breadth—name a period, style, or form, and it is represented. From Romanticism, Impressionism, and Judaica to photography, Pop Art, and Prairie School architecture and design, Mia has a tremendous scope that includes 100,000 pieces from 5,000 years of history. The museum expanded from its fledgling beginning in 1883 as the Minneapolis Society of Fine Arts with the construction of two additions in 1915. The range of art in the museum is immense, and because admission to the museum is free (with donations suggested), visitors can leisurely examine periods, styles, and techniques specific to their interests. The Agra Culture Coffee Shop and Café offer sustainably harvested treats and cold-press organic coffee, while the family area provides a place for kids to play, with hands-on activities that offer an artistic bent.

home is another Tudor Revival, originally built for milling mogul Charles S. Pillsbury, nephew of John; since 1993 it has housed the nonprofit BLIND Inc. (at 100 22nd St. E.).

Turn right on First Avenue South. The Institute for Agricultural and Trade Policy, a Georgian Revival–style building, appears on the right. The lovely brick house was built by notable local architect William Channing Whitney for Caroline Crosby, daughter of a founder of the company that later became General Mills. Across the street at the corner are nondescript neo-traditional condos that recently replaced a gas station on this site.

Turn right on Franklin Avenue East and take a look at the downtown Minneapolis skyline.

Turn right on Stevens Avenue South and continue down the block, where you'll see a wide array of housing stock on this block, ranging from modest to turn-of-the-20th-century luxurious.

Cross 22nd Street East and enter Washburn Fair Oaks Park. Proceed on the diagonal path southeast and enjoy the fresh air or take a seat on one of the many park benches.

Continue straight at the fork in the path.

The path ends at 24th Street East, where you can enjoy the splendor of the original 1916 Mia in proper perspective: a fine example of Classic Revival architecture designed by the then-influential New York firm of McKim, Mead, and White. The entrance stands out with its striking Ionian portico, complete with angels and Classic Chinese lions.

Turn around and follow the northeast path back to the starting point.

Points of Interest

1. **Washburn Fair Oaks Park** minneapolisparks.org, 200 24th St. E., Minneapolis, 612-230-6400

2. **Hennepin History Museum** hennepinhistory.org, 2303 Third Ave. S., Minneapolis, 612-870-1329

3. **Minneapolis Institute of Arts** artsmia.org, 2400 Third Ave. S., Minneapolis, 612-870-3132

4. **Children's Theatre Company** childrenstheatre.org, 2400 Third Ave. S., Minneapolis, 612-874-0400

5. **Minneapolis College of Art and Design** mcad.edu, 2501 Stevens Ave. S., Minneapolis, 612-874-3700

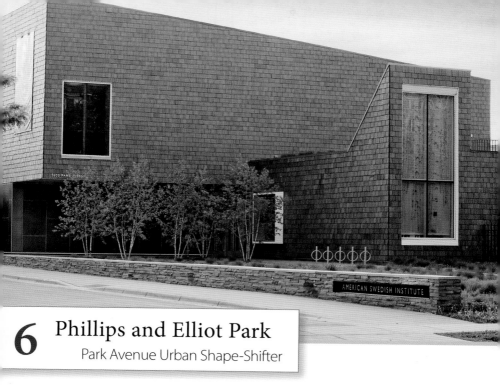

6 Phillips and Elliot Park
Park Avenue Urban Shape-Shifter

BOUNDARIES: 28th St. E., Portland Ave. S., Ninth St. S., Chicago Ave. S.
HUDSON'S TWIN CITIES STREET ATLAS COORDINATES: Map 394, 3C and 3D
DISTANCE: About 3.5 miles
DIFFICULTY: Easy
PARKING: Free parking on Park Ave. S.
PUBLIC TRANSIT: Bus lines 5, 9, and 11

The name Park Avenue conjures up images of the affluent street in New York City and elsewhere across the United States where the designation was used in obvious imitation. The Park Avenue area of Minneapolis was once the city's Victorian mansion row—much as Summit Avenue is in St. Paul, with more than 30 mansions between 18th and 28th Streets. However, Park Avenue suffered a different fate than Summit Avenue due to its easily accessible location directly south of downtown on flat prairie land. Instead of falling into disrepair and remaining so for decades, as its larger St. Paul counterpart did, Park Avenue was repeatedly redeveloped from 1890 to its 1920 heyday. Numerous great mansions on Park Avenue were razed, carved into apartments, or converted into homes for organizations such as the Ebenezer Church offices, the Shriners (Zuhrah Shrine Temple, 2540 Park Ave.), and social organizations such as chemical-dependency halfway houses and mental health treatment centers. The remaining Park Avenue mansions are most heavily concentrated in the Phillips neighborhood, while the north part of the walk heads into the Elliot Park neighborhood in the shadow of downtown. After losing almost half its population to freeway construction between 1950 and 1970, Elliot Park, today more affluent than Phillips, has become a hip hub for renovated and newly constructed apartments and condos.

Walk Description

Begin at the corner of 28th Street East and Park Avenue South. Observe the odd mixture of architecture that includes mansions, apartments, and functional corporate and organization buildings, such as the Ebenezer Corporate Offices and Park Apartments.

Head north on Park Avenue, crossing 27th Street East. Across the street is a local landmark and important cultural institution: the ❶ **American Swedish Institute** (ASI). The gaudy Château-esque and Baroque Revival beauty was constructed in 1908 for Swan J. Turnblad, publisher of the *Svenska Amerikanska Posten,* then the largest-selling Swedish-language newspaper in America. In 2012 ASI added the Nelson Cultural Center, featuring a gallery, an event center, a classroom offering Swedish-language and craft classes, and a new museum shop. The jewel of the new space is the café, Fika, which offers a selection of Swedish-inspired, reasonably priced gourmet cuisine.

Cross 26th Street East. On the left corner is the former Zuhrah Shrine Temple (1902), a lovely Italian Renaissance Revival mansion, now part of the ❷ **St. Mary's University** campus. Many old mansions here have been converted for new purposes, such as the various psychotherapy practices at Park Avenue Center and, across the street, the prosaic institutional buildings of St. Mary's University campus that fill more than two blocks.

Cross 25th Street East. On the right is Lemna Technologies (2445 Park Ave. S.). The building was originally the home of Anson and Georgia Brooks, who made their fortune in lumber but lived in a striking Venetian Gothic–style stone mansion.

Cross 24th Street East. On the right is where the greatest number of Victorian mansions for high-society Minneapolitans—including the home of James Ford Bell, the longtime head of General Mills—were demolished. Across the street are two mansions serving a new purpose. The Renaissance Revival George Peavey House (2222 Park Ave. S.) is now known as Freeport

Swan J. Turnblad's former mansion, now the American Swedish Institute

West Inc. The neighboring, colossal Romanesque Revival–style Sumner and Eugenie McKnight House (2200 Park Ave. S.) is currently occupied by American Indian Services.

Cross Franklin Avenue East, an area that was marred by drug dealers during the 1980s and '90s but has made a comeback in recent years due to diligent efforts and collaboration of local residents and the Minneapolis Police Department. On the left is ❸ **The Straitgate Church,** a massive brownstone church formerly known as Park Avenue Congregational.

Continue straight on Park Avenue South, crossing the bridge over I-94, which provides an alluring vantage point for downtown Minneapolis and the Elliot Park neighborhood in the immediate foreground. The next few blocks are in a state of flux as condos and redevelopment encroach; there are few single-family homes in this predominantly high-density, mixed-use area.

After crossing 14th Street East, follow Park Avenue South (Frontage Road) as it curves slightly to the right next to the redbrick Drexel Apartment Hotel. Turn right on 10th Street South. Ahead is a nice section of the neighborhood filled with businesses, condos, and apartments.

Turn left on 14th Street East. On the corner is the ❹ **Band Box Diner.** During the 1920s, the automobile became attainable for middle-income families and made possible this precursor to modern fast-food restaurants. The diner, which opened in 1929, mimicked the White Castle chain, serving inexpensive burgers and fries. One of 14 locations at the time, it sat vacant for years before reopening in 2003 to serve casual American fare.

Turn left on the corner of 14th Street East to head north on Chicago Avenue South, enjoying the view of downtown. Cross Centennial Place, where five city streets converge, and turn left on Ninth Street South. This street contains several of the city's most beautiful apartments, such as the Rappahannock—a huge stone building with wrought iron balconies, constructed in 1895.

Turn left on Portland Avenue South. This section of Elliot Park combines new and renovated condos. On the left are the Skyscape Condos. Continue on Portland, crossing 10th Street, an area lined with solid renovations, such as the Balmoral Apartments, and garish new constructions.

Cross 16th Street East. On the right is ❺ **Franklin Steele Square.** The small park was a gift from the daughters of the pioneer Steele, a pivotal leader in the early history of St. Anthony; it was annexed in 1872 by Minneapolis.

Cross I-94 and return to the Phillips neighborhood. Again, this area has improved over the past decade, but many homes are in need of renovation. Cross 19th Street East. On the left is ❻ **St. Paul's Evangelical Lutheran Church,** a Romanesque Revival gem constructed of brownstone and granite in 1889 and originally a Presbyterian church. The next block was once a haven for illegal drug sales and use. After demolition, some of the property has remained vacant, while condos and affordable apartments have been constructed on other lots.

Swan J. Turnblad: The American Dream—Swedish Style, and the Founding of the American Swedish Institute

Swan J. Turnblad was the embodiment of the Swedish American version of the American Dream. Born in rural Sweden, the youngest of 11 children, he immigrated in 1868 as a small child with his family to Vasa Township, the early Swedish settlement south of the Twin Cities. In 1879 he moved to Minneapolis, where he quickly rose as an important editor and publisher of Swedish-language newspapers, most notably the *Svenska Amerikanska Posten*. He purchased stock for the first issue in 1885, and by 1888 he owned and published the paper. Under his leadership, it grew from a faltering national Swedish-language paper to the undisputed leader by the 1890s. Even more important, by 1890 the number of Swedish immigrants in the United States had doubled from a decade before, to 478,000, with 21% living in Minnesota. Turnblad also engaged in real estate speculation, in part to buy property to develop a family home.

In 1903 he purchased six lots at 2600 Park Ave., where he would construct his enormous castlelike dream home, completed in 1908. Turnblad astutely realized that the Swedish-language demographic was aging, Americanizing, and shrinking, and he sold his newspaper in 1920. Turnblad died a few years later, but the organization he founded would become an astounding local and national success, with exhibits and other cultural events celebrating Swedish culture. In 2008 the former Turnblad mansion celebrated its 100th anniversary, and in 2012 the American Swedish Institute expanded to accommodate additional gallery space and Fika, a restaurant that serves "new Nordic" cuisine: espresso, salads, and award-winning *smörgås*, or open-faced sandwiches.

Turn left at the corner of Franklin Avenue East.

Turn right on Chicago Avenue South. On the left, approximately 0.5 mile down, at 15th Avenue South, was a tiny Romanian Jewish district at the turn of the 20th century until after World War II. On the right is ❼ **Peavey Field Park,** where you'll find sculptures and an abundance of park benches.

Continue south on Chicago Avenue South, where the new Minneapolis Grand Apartments are across the street from condemned and dilapidated homes.

Cross 25th Street East. On the left is the cheery architecture of Children's Hospitals and Clinics, which stands in stark contrast to the drab institutional look of the hospitals ahead.

Cross 27th Street East to walk through a neighborhood of huge, well-maintained Victorians.

Cross 28th Street East, turn right, and walk to the finish point at 28th Street and Park Avenue.

Phillips and Elliot Park

Points of Interest

1. **American Swedish Institute/Fika** asimn.org, 2600 Park Ave. S., Minneapolis, 612-871-4907
2. **St. Mary's University** smumn.edu, 2500 Park Ave., Minneapolis, 612-728-5100
3. **The Straitgate Church** straitgate.org, 638 Franklin Ave. E., Minneapolis, 612-870-7472
4. **Band Box Diner** facebook.com/bandboxeats, 729 10th St. S., Minneapolis, 612-332-0850
5. **Franklin Steele Square** minneapolisparks.org, 1600 Portland Ave. S., Minneapolis, 612-230-6400
6. **St. Paul's Evangelical Lutheran Church** stpaulsevlutheran.org, 1901 Portland Ave. S., Minneapolis, 612-874-0133
7. **Peavey Field Park** minneapolisparks.org, 730 22nd St. E., Minneapolis, 612-230-6400

7 Loring Park and the Walker Art Center
Art and Nature at a Nexus

Above: *View of the Minneapolis skyline across Loring Lake in autumn*

BOUNDARIES: Oak Grove St./15th St. W., Vineland Pl., Dunwoody Blvd., Willow St.
HUDSON'S TWIN CITIES STREET ATLAS COORDINATES: Map 394, 1C and 2C
DISTANCE: About 1 mile
DIFFICULTY: Easy
PARKING: 2-hour metered parking on Willow St.; paid parking at the Walker Art Center
    parking ramp on Vineland Pl.
PUBLIC TRANSIT: Bus lines 6, 17, and 18

Loring Park and the Walker Art Center seamlessly integrate artsy aesthetic with earthy utilitarian-ism. This is the place for contemporary art in all media, as well as the place for reflecting on and basking in the wealth of nature. Despite its geographic shortcomings (several major roads bisect the park and the art center), the beauty of the area's architecture and green space supplants the nearby freeway's din. The Irene Hixon Whitney Bridge (1988) is a crucial element in creating this environment: the pedestrian and bicycle span crosses 16 lanes of traffic yet provides a panoramic view of the exquisite surroundings while linking the park and the works of art. Both institutions are rooted in Minneapolis's early rise to national prominence; the Walker Art Center takes its name from Thomas Walker, a local lumberman turned art collector and philanthropist. His original museum was constructed near the present-day site in 1927, but it was replaced with the much larger modernist structure by Edward Barnes Larrabee in 1971. Then in 2005, the Walker expanded again—this time, noted Swiss architects Jacques Herzog and Pierre de Meuron added 130,000 square feet along Hennepin Avenue. In June 2017, the new Minneapolis Sculpture Garden and Walker Art Center grounds opened, with 60 sculptures—20 of them new—across 19 acres.

Loring Park has an equally important history: it opened in 1883 as Central Park and was modeled on the world-famous park of the same name in New York City—despite the fact that Minneapolis's version is central to nothing in the city. The 35-acre park and the picturesque lake (formerly Johnson Lake) were later renamed in honor of the city's first park board commissioner, flour-milling magnate Charles Loring. Complementing the artistic, natural, and civil-engineered beauty of the area is an abundance of moderately priced fine-dining establishments—many with alfresco patios and rooftop tables during warm-weather months.

Walk Description

Begin at the northeast corner of Oak Grove Street and Hennepin Avenue. Looking up the hill to the left, you'll see two of the finest examples of church architecture in the city, both designed by Minneapolis architect Edwin Hewitt. Immediately across the street on the left is ❶ **St. Mark's Episcopal Cathedral** (1911). Hewitt was a member of this parish, and the building was inspired by English Gothic style and Magdalen College at Oxford. St. Mark's began as a parish church but was elevated to a cathedral in 1941. Farther south on Hennepin Avenue is the 238-foot spire of ❷ **Hennepin Avenue United Methodist Church.** The Gothic-inspired church was designed in 1916 by Hewitt and his brother-in-law.

Between the two churches are the 510 Groveland Apartments; the Renaissance Revival building now houses condos. Another perspective that highlights the magnitude of the architecture on this block is from the Irene Hixon Whitney Bridge.

Continue straight, carefully crossing Hennepin Avenue and Lyndale Avenue. Across the street is ❸ **Walker Art Center,** a national leader in contemporary visual and performing arts. The Walker has a diverse permanent collection and hosts traveling exhibitions that have included works by Frida Kahlo and Pablo Picasso. In addition, dance, films, music, and classes are available at the august art institution. The Walker's restaurant, ❹ **Esker Grove,** is operated by chef Doug Flicker, whose elegant dishes specialize in local, sustainably sourced ingredients. Its large picture window and patio offer a beautiful view of the Walker Sculpture Garden, located just outside.

At the first set of stairs between the paired pillars, go down into the park. The profusion of sculptures in the free public gallery is staggering and worthy of hours of examination.

Turn left at the first through gravel pathway to the Cowles Pavilion, and then turn right on the concrete path.

Turn right and continue straight, passing *Spoonbridge and Cherry,* the most recognizable piece of public art in the Twin Cities.

Basilica of Saint Mary

After exploring the sculpture garden, continue east to cross the Irene Hixon Whitney Bridge toward Loring Park. The bridge provides an incredible scenic vista above Hennepin Avenue. Below is the first part of the walk, as well as downtown Minneapolis, the Walker Art Center, and ❺ **Loring Park,** from a unique perspective. On the left is the nearby ❻ **Basilica of Saint Mary,** an enormous Beaux arts procathedral (or secondary cathedral) for the archdiocese of St. Paul and Minneapolis.

Follow the stairs down to the innermost path at Loring Lake, and turn left. Across the street from the park on the left is the Fawkes Building, originally an auto dealership from 1911 to 1917. Today it's home to several restaurants and businesses, including the upscale comfort-food restaurant ❼ **Café Lurcat.**

Turn left near the lake, where you can perch on a park bench and observe the ducks, geese, orioles, cattails, and reeds in this natural environment surrounded by a quaint urban setting.

Follow the curve around the lake. On the left are additional Loring Park businesses, featuring another fine restaurant with outdoor dining:

The Minneapolis Sculpture Garden: Fine Art in an Outside Environment

The Twin Cities provide a wealth of opportunities for appreciating the intersection of nature and art: the Minneapolis Sculpture Garden is the best example. Comprising 40 permanent works of art—even before the planned expansion—the museum's art, arbor, and bridge are on view thanks to a collaboration between the Walker Art Center and the Minneapolis Park and Recreation Board. Of course, the best-known public art is *Spoonbridge and Cherry* (1985–89), by husband-and-wife pop art sculptors Claes Oldenburg and Coosje Van Bruggen. The splashiest recent acquisition is *Hahn/Cock,* a 10-foot-tall fiberglass blue chicken that dominates the new north entrance. Artist Katharina Fritsch alters the recognizable with changes in color and scale to bring new insights to everyday objects. Another recognizable piece is *Love,* by Robert Indiana. The sculpture is one version of many of the same work by the world-famous pop artist—this time in steel. The sculpture garden, which opened in 1988, has expanded from the original 4-acre site that formerly featured the Tyrone Guthrie Theater, planned by the late University of Minnesota architect and professor Ralph Rapson. The 2016 renovation of the sculpture garden includes multiple new entries, a new 5-acre upper garden, a new main lobby, and plenty of new plantings and green space.

❽ 4 Bells, a seafood restaurant with a menu that includes oysters on the half shell, fresh fish, and shellfish flown in daily from both coasts, not to mention a splendid rooftop view.

Continue, passing the gardens and the bridge as the path veers left. The landscape architecture is stunning, with the benches and flowers arranged in a circle—each bench provides another panoramic vantage point of the city. Follow the path along the irregular shape of the lake as it curves slightly right.

Turn right as the path continues past the basketball court, playground, and Mission Revival–style Loring Park Community Center (1906), all on the left.

Turn right at the bend and follow the contour of the lake. On the left across 15th Street are several beautiful pieces of architecture, including the rear of the Renaissance Revival–style **❾ Woman's Club of Minneapolis** (1927), which continues to host lectures and concerts here.

Turn left at the fork in the path. Then turn right and proceed to finish the walk at the intersection of Hennepin Avenue and Oak Grove Street.

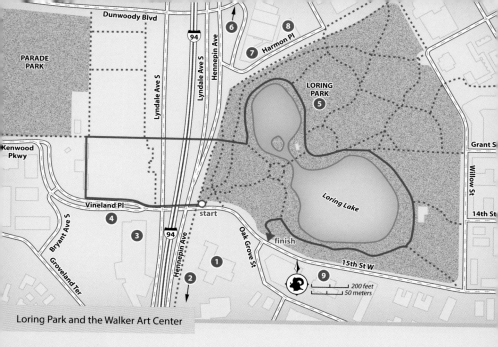

Loring Park and the Walker Art Center

Points of Interest

1. **St. Mark's Episcopal Cathedral** ourcathedral.org, 519 Oak Grove St., Minneapolis, 612-870-7800

2. **Hennepin Avenue United Methodist Church** hennepinchurch.org, 511 Groveland Ave., Minneapolis, 612-871-5303

3. **Walker Art Center** walkerart.org, 1750 Hennepin Ave., Minneapolis, 612-375-7622

4. **Esker Grove** eskergrove.com, 723 Vineland Place, Minneapolis, 612-375-3540

5. **Loring Park** minneapolisparks.org, 1382 Willow St., Minneapolis, 612-370-4929

6. **The Basilica of Saint Mary** mary.org, 88 17th St. N., Minneapolis, 612-333-1381

7. **Café Lurcat** cafelurcat.com, 1624 Harmon Pl., Minneapolis, 612-486-5500

8. **4 Bells** 4bells.com, 1610 Harmon Pl., Minneapolis, 612-904-1163

9. **The Woman's Club of Minneapolis** womansclub.org, 410 Oak Grove St., Minneapolis, 612-870-8001

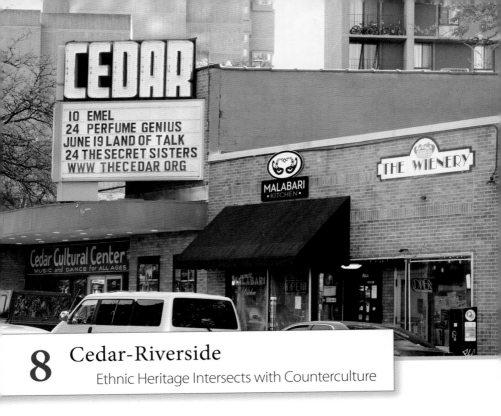

8 Cedar-Riverside
Ethnic Heritage Intersects with Counterculture

Above: Cedar Cultural Center, ground zero for world and eclectic music acts

BOUNDARIES: Franklin Ave. E., 15th Ave. S., Third St. S., 19th Ave. S.
HUDSON'S TWIN CITIES STREET ATLAS COORDINATES: Map 394, 3C and 4C
DISTANCE: About 1.75 miles
DIFFICULTY: Easy
PARKING: 2-hour metered parking on 19th Ave. S. and Franklin Frontage Rd.;
   metered parking on Franklin Ave.
PUBLIC TRANSIT: Bus lines 2, 3, and 7; Metro Blue Line at Franklin Ave. Station

Cedar-Riverside has an enduring history as one of the Twin Cities' great ethnic salad bowls. It has also been an exemplar of a combined commercial and residential area, albeit for the working class or working poor, throughout each historic epoch. The triangle-shaped community is nestled between the Mississippi River, the University of Minnesota (U of M), and two important interstate highways, I-35W and I-94. Diverse groups of people over the years have resided and shopped in the area sometimes referred to as the West Bank. Scandinavians dominated the neighborhood, particularly the business district on Cedar Avenue, from the 1890s until the Great Depression. The neighborhood seriously declined after World War II. Large portions of its decaying housing were demolished to make room for interstate highways and the expansion of U of M on the west bank of the Mississippi River in the 1960s. The proximity to U of M and inexpensive housing inspired a burgeoning counterculture. The various modalities of the area's hippie past are readily apparent in the restaurants and stores—many originating from the early '70s punks, radicals, and reformers turned businesspeople. Since the early 1990s, immigrant groups, particularly the Somalis, have moved into the neighborhood's rental units and have created their own thriving businesses. The Cedar-Riverside community has become increasingly appealing because of its diversity—a neighborhood of old hippies, college kids, and recent immigrants—and easy accessibility by the Metro Blue Line. Genuine counterculture and ongoing immigration history come alive on the streets of Cedar-Riverside.

Walk Description

Start at the Franklin Avenue Station and turn right on the combined pedestrian and bicycle path that runs parallel with the light-rail transit line.

Continue on this path, absorbing the numerous scenic vistas of Minneapolis en route to the Cedar-Riverside Station. To the left is the light-rail transit garage, and just past I-94 is the colossal Riverside Plaza (1973), formerly Cedar Square West Apartments. The complex was part of the first federally supported urban New Town. Ralph Rapson, a University of Minnesota architecture professor, designed the modernist apartments—some with 1,300 units that exceed 40 stories and stretch over 11 blocks. The slightly ominous structure experienced financial difficulties, filed bankruptcy, and was sold in the 1980s by the City of Minneapolis. The apartments are now home to numerous immigrants, especially Somalis.

Cross the street at the crosswalk and turn right immediately on 15th Avenue South. On your left is ❶ Currie Park, I-35W, the U.S. Bank Stadium, and downtown.

Turn right on Fifth Street South and then left on 15th Avenue South. After passing the park, you'll see the Brian Coyle Community Center across the street. It serves neighborhood youth, families, and immigrants and is named for the late three-term Minneapolis city councilman, who was a strong advocate for human rights, housing, and the environment, as well as the rights of gay, lesbian, and transgender populations. Coyle died of AIDS in 1991.

Turn right on Fourth Street South at the ❷ **Mixed Blood Theatre,** which was founded in 1976 by 22-year-old Jack Reuler. Since then it has produced a culturally pluralistic arts organization, though specializing in plays, in a renovated fire station.

Turn left on Cedar Avenue South. Across the street is ❸ **Midwest Mountaineering,** the store for climbing, camping, paddling, travel, and all outdoors activities since 1970. The hippie-owned business moved to its present location in 1976 in the transitional counterculture hotbed, where it has expanded five times to better serve the outdoors adventurer.

Turn right on Third Street South. Appropriately located down the stairs in the basement of Midwest Mountaineering is ❹ **Mayday Books,** a volunteer collective nonprofit dedicated to selling progressive literature and magazines.

Turn right on 19th Avenue South. Across the street is the ❺ **University of Minnesota** and its Hubert H. Humphrey Institute of Public Affairs and Carlson School of Management.

Turn right on Riverside Avenue. Across the street is the ❻ **Hard Times Cafe,** a cooperatively owned restaurant and coffee shop open 22 hours a day to serve members of the counterculture,

Mayday Books, purveyor of progressive literature

Cedar Avenue: Minneapolis's Snoose Boulevard

During its early history, Cedar-Riverside was one of America's great "Snoose Boulevards." It took its name from the teeming masses of Scandinavian immigrants who visited the area for the many social activities along Cedar Avenue South from the 1890s until the early 20th century. "Snoose Boulevard" was a pejorative term coined by old-stock Americans aimed at denouncing the popular Scandinavian habit of chewing tobacco, or *snuset*, especially by working men in the milling and lumber industries.

Built by the local Danish community, Dania Hall (1886) was the center of Scandinavian vaudeville and kept it thriving until the Depression. It would not recover as the Scandinavian population aged and moved from the neighborhood. The building was sold in 1963, and in 2000, after years of neglect and efforts to rebuild the landmark, it was destroyed by a fire.

Snoose Boulevard is in Cedar-Riverside's distant past, but the legacy continues in the waves of new immigrants living in the vast Riverside Plaza apartment buildings and walking Cedar Avenue today. The new, hardworking immigrants share the American Dream to improve their lives and those of their children while shaping institutions and businesses in the neighborhood to serve their communities.

from hippie to punk. On the right is the Bailey Building, home to KFAI (90.3 FM in Minneapolis or 106.7 FM in St. Paul), which provides community radio and a diverse voice for music and talk. On the corner is ❼ **Acadia Café,** relocated from Eat Street (Nicollet Avenue) to this large space. In the move, they've brought their eclectic nightly music schedule as well as a wide selection of beers on tap (28!), plus coffee, burgers, and sandwiches.

Turn left on Cedar Avenue South. Across the street is one of the Twin Cities' best dive restaurants: ❽ **The Wienery,** where they have perfected the art of the hot dog (including a tasty vegan version). A few doors down is the ❾ **Cedar Cultural Center,** the Twin Cities' premier venue for world music since 1991.

On the left is a vacant lot that used to house Dania Hall, the beloved site of Scandinavian vaudeville that was boarded up for years before it burned down in 2000.

Turn right after crossing Sixth Street South, and turn left after crossing Cedar Avenue South. Carefully walk under the I-94 overpass. On the right are the ❿ **Community Peace Gardens.**

Continue to follow Cedar Avenue to the Franklin Avenue Station to finish the walk.

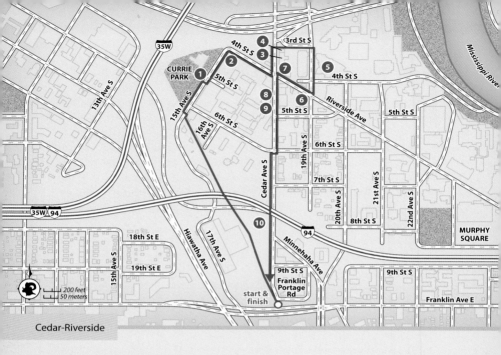

Points of Interest

1. **Currie Park** minneapolisparks.org, 500 15th Ave. S., Minneapolis, 612-230-6400

2. **Mixed Blood Theatre** mixedblood.com, 1501 Fourth St. S., Minneapolis, 612-338-0937

3. **Midwest Mountaineering** midwestmtn.com, 309 Cedar Ave. S., Minneapolis, 612-339-3433

4. **Mayday Books** maydaybookstore.org, 301 Cedar Ave. S., Minneapolis, 612-333-4719

5. **University of Minnesota** umn.edu/twincities, 321 19th Ave. S., Minneapolis, 612-625-2008

6. **Hard Times Cafe** hardtimes.com, 1821 Riverside Ave., Minneapolis, 612-341-9261

7. **Acadia Café** acadiapub.com, 329 Cedar Ave. S., Minneapolis, 612-874-8702

8. **The Wienery** wienery.com, 414 Cedar Ave. S., Minneapolis, 612-333-5798

9. **Cedar Cultural Center** thecedar.org, 416 Cedar Ave. S., Minneapolis, 612-338-2674

10. **Community Peace Gardens** sites.google.com/site/commpeacegarden/home, 808 Cedar Ave. S., Minneapolis, 612-342-1344, ext. 5

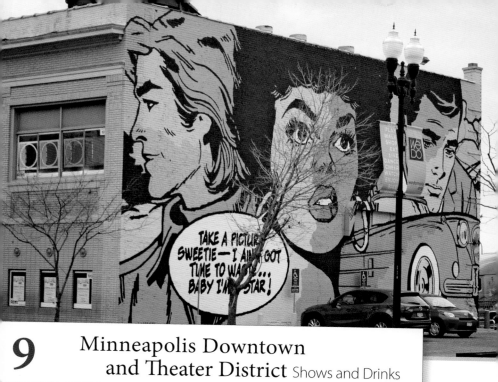

9 Minneapolis Downtown and Theater District Shows and Drinks

Above: Mural by Greg Gossel on the old National Camera Exchange building

BOUNDARIES: 10th St. N., First Ave. N., Fourth St. N., Hennepin Ave.
HUDSON'S TWIN CITIES STREET ATLAS COORDINATES: Map 394, 2B
DISTANCE: About 1 mile
DIFFICULTY: Easy
PARKING: Limited street parking and parking ramps on First Ave. N. or Fifth St. N.
PUBLIC TRANSIT: Multiple bus lines; light rail

The Twin Cities are second only to New York City in live theater performances and attendance per capita, and nowhere is this more apparent than in downtown Minneapolis's Theater District. Since the 1920s, the Orpheum, State, and Pantages Theatres have opened their stages to the likes of the Marx Brothers, Jack Benny, George Burns, and Gracie Allen, and, more recently, to live productions of *The Lion King*—which premiered at the Orpheum—and *The Graduate*, starring Kathleen Turner. All three venues also offer great live music and comedy, with touring acts as varied as Margaret Cho, Eric Idle, Bebel Gilberto, and Modest Mouse. This walk takes you through the historic neighborhood, as well as all the cool places to hang out before and after theater events.

Walk Description

Start at First Avenue North and Fifth Street North. The light-rail train goes down Fifth Street to the station to your left (southeast) from here. Pick up a route schedule at the station for future use.

Cross Fifth Street North to follow First Avenue North. On your left is a charming mural that spans the side of the fantastic ❶ **Gluek's Restaurant & Bar.** In operation since 1933, it's the oldest restaurant in downtown Minneapolis. Aside from their small but wonderful trans fat–free menu, this is the best place to buy a mug of rich and creamy Gluek's beer.

Cross Seventh Street North. Directly in front of you is the star-covered ❷ **First Avenue** nightclub, which for more than 30 years has brought in acts as diverse as Iggy Pop, Ice-T, and Stereolab. You may recognize it from scenes in Prince's film *Purple Rain,* and if not, you'll probably recognize many of the club's past performers, whose names are spray-painted on the stars covering the building.

Turn left to follow Seventh Street North and walk alongside First Avenue nightclub. The small door leading into the side of the building is the club's smaller "subclub," the 7th Street Entry, which brings many international touring bands to a more intimate setting and also features good local bands just starting out. Right next door to 7th Street Entry is First Avenue's newest addition, The Depot Tavern.

Turn right on Hennepin Avenue. On your right is the ❸ **Pantages Theatre.** Past Eighth Street is the recently relocated ❹ **Brave New Workshop,** a comedy institution founded by Dudley Riggs, a former Ringling Bros. and Barnum & Bailey aerialist who created the organization's precursor, the Instant Theatre in New York City. After touring with that group, Riggs moved to Minneapolis in the 1950s and changed the name. Fifty-plus years after it was founded, it continues its mission with comedy shows, stand-up, and improv. ❺ **The Saloon** and the former Amsterdam Hotel upstairs are some of the last remnants from the area's notorious past of prostitution and clandestine, pre-Stonewall gay bars. The Saloon is famous for mixing some of the strongest drinks in town. Next door is the ❻ **Orpheum Theatre.**

Take a left at 10th Street North to cross Hennepin Avenue. The giant church on your left is the ❼ **First Baptist Church,** built in 1885.

Take an immediate left to go back up Hennepin on the other side of the street.

Cross Ninth Street. This takes you right past the beautiful ❽ **State Theatre.** The now-defunct Skyway Show Lounge was where Diablo Cody, the author of *Candy Girl* and *Juno,* worked briefly as a stripper.

Cross Seventh Street. On the left is the former Hennepin Center for the Arts, now a part of ❾ **The Cowles Center for Dance & the Performing Arts,** located inside a gigantic former Masonic temple built in 1889. Within the building's eight floors reside more than 17 performing and visual art companies. Next door is the historic Shubert Theatre.

Cross Fifth Street. To your right is the massive Lumber Exchange Building. Built in 1885, it's the oldest building taller than 12 stories outside of New York City and the first building to be billed as fireproof in the country. On the left is ❿ **Gay 90's,** the largest gay and lesbian entertainment complex in the upper Midwest, with eight bars, two restaurants, a drag lounge, a male strip show, a leather-only bar, and three huge dance floors. It also has a bingo night.

Gay 90's entertainment complex

Turn left onto Fourth Street North and cross Hennepin Avenue. Just ahead on the left ⓫ **Clockwerks Brewing** serves excellent craft beer in a steampunk Victorian setting. Go straight to the corner of First Avenue North and Fourth Street North. Turn left to go to Fifth Street North, the starting point.

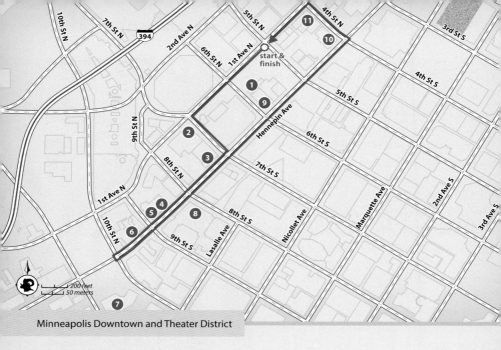

Minneapolis Downtown and Theater District

Points of Interest

1. **Gluek's Restaurant & Bar** glueks.com, 16 Sixth Street N., Minneapolis, 612-338-6621

2. **First Avenue and 7th Street Entry/The Depot Tavern** first-avenue.com, 701 First Ave. N., Minneapolis, 612-332-1775

3. **Pantages Theatre** hennepintheatretrust.org, 710 Hennepin Ave., Minneapolis, 612-373-5600

4. **Brave New Workshop** theatre.bravenewworkshop.com, 824 Hennepin Ave., Minneapolis, 612-332-6620

5. **The Saloon** saloonmn.com, 830 Hennepin Ave., Minneapolis, 612-288-0459

6. **Orpheum Theatre** hennepintheatretrust.org, 910 Hennepin Ave., Minneapolis, 612-339-7007

7. **First Baptist Church** fbcminneapolis.org, 1021 Hennepin Ave., Minneapolis, 612-332-3651

8. **State Theatre** hennepintheatretrust.org, 805 Hennepin Ave., Minneapolis, 612-339-7007

9. **The Cowles Center for Dance & the Performing Arts** thecowlescenter.org, 528 Hennepin Ave., Minneapolis, 612-206-3636

10. **Gay 90's** gay90s.com, 408 Hennepin Ave., Minneapolis, 612-333-7755

11. **Clockwerks Brewing** clockwerksbrewing.com, 25 Fourth Street N., Minneapolis, 612-339-9375

10 Downtown/Washington Avenue
A New Focus for an Old Neighborhood

Above: The Guthrie Theater

BOUNDARIES: Third St. S., Third Ave. S., Second St. S., 12th Ave. S.
HUDSON'S TWIN CITIES STREET ATLAS COORDINATES: Map 394, 3B
DISTANCE: About 1.75 miles
DIFFICULTY: Easy
PARKING: Metered parking on Second St. S.
PUBLIC TRANSIT: Bus lines 2, 3, 7, and 17

The Downtown neighborhood, just off the Mill District, is another area in flux. Less than 20 years ago, it consisted mostly of abandoned warehouse buildings, machine shops, and lots of parking ramps. The big white bubble of the Metrodome has been replaced by the massive "Viking ship" of U.S. Bank Stadium as the key point of interest.

Today, this neighborhood is home to one of the largest literary collectives in the country and a world-renowned theater, as well as upscale restaurants, publishing houses, and architectural firms. A walk down Washington Avenue means a stroll among old railroad beds converted into parking lots, as well as candy factories and meatpacking plants converted into performance spaces for National Endowment for the Arts prize–winning poets and writers. Multiuse condos and apartments will soon fill every vacant lot as downtown Minneapolis and the Mississippi River experience a renaissance—to the point that condo growth has inspired real estate developers to rechristen parts, or all, of the area "Downtown East."

Walk Description

Start on the corner of Fifth Avenue South and Second Street South with the MacPhail Center for Music at your back. Walk past the Residence Inn by Marriott, formerly the Milwaukee Road Depot—built in 1899 and in use until 1971. Now, the spacious building comprises not only a hotel but also a great indoor water park open to non–hotel guests for a fee. Even though locals still fume that the more glamorous Union Depot, formerly located near the Hennepin Avenue Bridge, wasn't preserved as well, it's still nice that this lovely old building, with its attached clock tower and ornate boarding platform, has been saved from the wrecking ball. Ahead and to your right is the Carlyle Condos building, the tallest residential building in Minneapolis.

Turn left at Third Avenue South. On the corner is ❶ **Dunn Brothers Coffee,** located in the original freight house serving the Milwaukee Road Depot. This Dunn Brothers sells great coffee drinks and pastries and regularly hosts live music. On the right at 220 Washington Ave. South is the United States Federal Office Building, which briefly served as the city's main post office.

Turn left at Washington Avenue South to head southeast. Across the street is ❷ **Eastside,** which serves American cuisine with a heavy seafood emphasis. Continue straight, past the depot and its elegant, covered boarding platform, which now serves as a parking lot for hotel guests.

Cross Fifth Avenue South. On your left is Colombian figural artist Fernando Botero's bronze sculpture of two portly nudes dancing. Cross the street at Portland Avenue South, and continue walking on the other side of Washington Avenue South. On your left is ❸ **Zen Box Izakaya,** an excellent restaurant specializing in Japanese comfort food.

Cross Park Avenue South and continue southeast. On the left side of the street, the reno-vated old lumber, textile, and flour mill ruins—now glitzy condos—provide a wonderful glimpse of the area's past and present. The building with the big star on top is the former North Star Woolen Mill, while the Washburn A Mill and Ceresota Flour buildings have retained the original faded logos painted on their sides. The building with the giant crater on top is the ❹ **Mill City Museum** (see Walk 13). To the left is the blue curve of the ❺ **Guthrie Theater,** a bastion of Twin

Cities' live theater since 1963, and at this particular location since 2006.

The big brick building at 1011 Washington Ave. S. is **❻ Open Book,** which houses the largest literary collective in the country. Inside are the Minnesota Center for the Book Arts, which offers classes on bookmaking; the Loft Literary Center, a creative-writing school; and a coffee shop that sells soups, sandwiches, and pastries. **❼ Grumpy's** is a great bar and restaurant owned by former Halo of Flies front man and Amphetamine Reptile Records owner Tom Hazelmyer.

Turn right at 12th Avenue, and go straight and turn right at the stop sign to follow Third Street.

Cross 10th Avenue South and cut through the parking lot, angling to the left. Across the street is the **❽ U.S. Bank Stadium,** home of the Minnesota Vikings football team.

Cross Norm McGrew Place/Ninth Avenue South and walk straight. Ahead

The Open Book building, home of the Loft Literary Center and Minnesota Center for the Book Arts

is downtown Minneapolis. To the right, you can see most of the old Mill District on either side of the river, as well as the Guthrie Theater. Ahead and to the left you'll see the big arched roof of the Minneapolis Armory, where the Minnesota Lakers played basketball before moving to Los Angeles in the 1960s.

Cross Fifth Avenue South, and then turn right to follow it. Cross Washington Avenue South and go straight. On the right is the **❾ MacPhail Center for Music,** a school for young musicians. The school holds regular lunchtime concerts that are free and open to the public—an easy thing to appreciate, even if you don't have kids attending the school. Up ahead is Second Street South and Fifth Avenue South, our starting point.

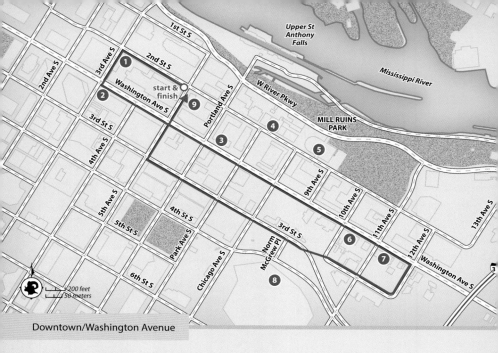

Downtown/Washington Avenue

Points of Interest

1. **Dunn Brothers Coffee** dunnbrothers.com, 201 Third Ave. S., Minneapolis, 612-692-8530

2. **Eastside** eastsidempls.com, 305 Washington Ave. S., Minneapolis, 612-208-1638

3. **Zen Box Izakaya,** zenbox.com, 602 Washington Ave. S., Minneapolis, 612-332-3936

4. **Mill City Museum** millcitymuseum.org, 704 Second St. S., Minneapolis, 612-341-7555

5. **Guthrie Theater** guthrietheater.org, 818 Second St. S., Minneapolis, 612-377-2224

6. **Open Book** openbookmn.org, 1011 Washington Ave. S., Ste. 100, Minneapolis, 612-215-2520

7. **Grumpy's** grumpys-bar.com/downtown.html, 1111 Washington Ave. S., Minneapolis, 612-340-9738

8. **U.S. Bank Stadium** usbankstadium.com, 401 Chicago Ave., Minneapolis, 612-777-8700

9. **MacPhail Center for Music** macphail.org, 501 Second St. S., Minneapolis, 612-321-0100

11 Warehouse District/North Loop
The Oldest "New" Neighborhood

Above: *View of the downtown extension of the Cedar Lake Trail*

BOUNDARIES: First Ave. N., Fourth St. N., 10th Ave. N., Washington Ave. N.
HUDSON'S TWIN CITIES STREET ATLAS COORDINATES: Map 394, 2B
DISTANCE: About 2 miles
DIFFICULTY: Moderate
PARKING: Metered parking on Washington Ave.
PUBLIC TRANSIT: Bus lines 4, 6, 7, 12, 14, and 61

With the completion of the transcontinental railroad systems in the 1860s, Minneapolis became an important wholesale trade center for the country. By the early 1920s, more than 300 warehouse businesses, including paper, paint, and farm machinery manufacturers, were located here in Minneapolis, and with these new businesses came lots of money. Some of the greatest architects of the day were hired to design these buildings, and they did so with flair.

The North Loop neighborhood of Minneapolis's Warehouse District features an amazingly intact concentration of late-19th- to early-20th-century commercial buildings, spared from the wrecking ball not from any appreciation of the architecture but simply because the city couldn't afford to demolish the buildings. Today, these buildings have been converted into remarkable condos, restaurants, and nightclubs. Target Field, home of the Twins baseball team, has influenced the area's development, especially along the Cedar Lake Trail downtown bicycle path.

Walk Description

Start at the TractorWorks Building (800–828 Washington Ave. N.), built in 1902. Decorated with a large high relief stag head over the entrance, it served as the Minneapolis headquarters for the farm-implement company John Deere. .Go straight to follow Washington Avenue northeast. Cross 10th Avenue North and turn left to follow 10th Avenue North southwest.

Turn left at Third Street North and go straight, heading southeast. Some of the better condo developments in recent years are here: 918 Lofts (918 Third St. N.) and Bassett Creek Lofts (901 Third St. N.).

Cross Eighth Avenue North and continue southeast. On the corner you'll find the fenced-in ❶ North Loop Dog Grounds. On the right side of the street (701 Third St. N.) is Sherwin-Williams's ornate former Minneapolis headquarters building. Throughout this area you'll notice hints of the huge paper-milling district once here, including the C. J. Duffey Paper Company, Litin Paper Company, Falk Paper Company, and the *Star Tribune*'s paper-manufacturing building.

Cross Sixth Avenue North and go straight. Across the street (525 Third St. N.) is the Bookmen Loft Condo building—originally the Bookmen Printing Building. On this side of the street is ❷ Corner Coffee, which serves up live acoustic music with its coffee and food, for lunch and for late-night crowds, Monday–Saturday.

Turn right on Fifth Avenue North. ❸ Modist Brewing Co. brews a variety of award-winning beers in a spacious, art-centric warehouse setting.

Just after the stop sign at Fourth Street North, turn left to take the sidewalk that goes under the I-94 on-ramp. (If you're thirsty, turn right, following the underpass sidewalk, and turn left on Sixth Avenue. On your right, half a block away, you'll see the ❹ Fulton Brewery Tap Room.) Off to your right is the Twins baseball stadium, ❺ Target Field, completed in 2010. Below you are both defunct and working train tracks and a light-rail stop for the stadium, while to your left is a panoramic view of the Warehouse District.

Follow the path down to Second Avenue North and cross the street. Turn right to head southwest on Second Avenue North.

Turn left at Fourth Street North. Across the street is the historic Textile Building, built in 1891, where you'll find local favorite restaurant **❻ Pizza Lucé.** At the corner and on the right is the spectacularly ornate Wyman Building at 400 First Ave. N., built in 1896. Until recently, it was occupied by local artists and private gallery owners, but due to rising rental costs, the building is now occupied mostly by architectural firms, real estate investors, and upscale bars.

Turn left at First Avenue North. On your left is the gray stone hulk of the Consortium Building, built in 1887. At 241 First Ave. N. is the Lerner Publishing Group, a successful publisher of children's books that has resided at this address since 1959.

Turn left at Washington Avenue North. **❼ One on One Bicycle Studio** is a live-music venue and art gallery that serves coffee drinks and even runs a bicycle repair shop in the back. The gigantic brick building near the corner houses **❽ Sex World,** one of the largest sex shops in the country and home of one of the first Internet coffee shops in the city. It's now at risk of gentrification as the neighborhood continues to evolve from industrial wasteland.

Cross the street. To the left is **❾ Red Rabbit,** a Minnesota version of New York–style, red-and-white-tablecloth Italian cuisine, with huge portions at reasonable prices.

Cross the iron railroad bridge and continue northwest. You're now in the middle of the Warehouse District/North Loop neighborhood—and in a fabulous picture-taking spot. On the right, the Free Spirit building (428 Washington Ave. N.) is home to Free Spirit Publishing, another award-winning publisher of children's books. On the right is **❿ Black Sheep,** an East Coast–style, coal-fired pizzeria. On your left is **⓫ Smack Shack,** home of all things lobster. Its trademark lobster roll sandwich was named one of the best in the country by *Bon Appétit*—not bad, considering that Minneapolis is well over a thousand miles away from any lobster traps. On the right is the International Harvester Company of America building (618 Washington Ave. N.), built in 1916 and a former distribution site for farm machinery. It's now the Harvester Lofts, an upscale condo development. At 701 Washington Ave. N. is the former factory building for Loose-Wiles Biscuit Company; built in 1910, it features a gorgeously menacing stone lion over the entranceway. **⓬ JUN,** on the 700 block, features fine Szechuan food and daily dim sum.

Cross Eighth Avenue North. Across the street is the TractorWorks Building, where you'll finish the walk.

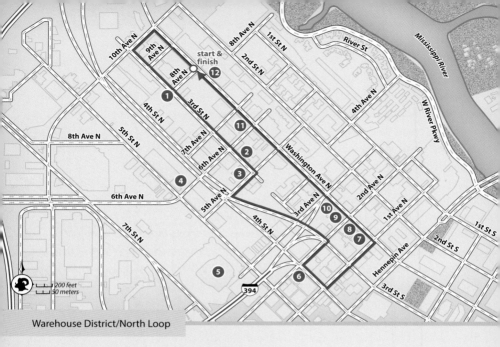

Warehouse District/North Loop

Points of Interest

1. **North Loop Dog Grounds** doggrounds.com, Third St. N. and Eighth Ave. N., Minneapolis

2. **Corner Coffee** corner.coffee/northloop, 514 Third St. N., #102, Minneapolis, 612-338-2002

3. **Modist Brewing Co.** modistbrewing.com, 505 Third St. N., Minneapolis, 612-454-0258

4. **Fulton Brewery Tap Room** fultonbeer.com, 414 Sixth Ave. N., Minneapolis, 612-333-3208

5. **Target Field** twinsbaseball.com, 1 Twins Way, Minneapolis, 612-338-9467

6. **Pizza Lucé** pizzaluce.com, 119 Fourth St. N., Minneapolis, 612-333-7359

7. **One on One Bicycle Studio** oneononebike.com, 117 Washington Ave. N., Minneapolis, 612-371-9565

8. **Sex World** shopsexworld.com, 241 Second Ave. N., Minneapolis, 612-672-0556

9. **Red Rabbit** redrabbitmn.com, 201 Washington Ave. N., Minneapolis, 612-767-8855

10. **Black Sheep** blacksheeppizza.com, 600 Washington Ave. N., Minneapolis, 612-342-2625

11. **Smack Shack** smack-shack.com, 603 Washington Ave. N., Minneapolis, 612-379-4322

12. **JUN** junnorthloop.com, 730 Washington Ave. N., Minneapolis, 612-208-0706

12 Bridge Square, the Gateway, Boom Island, Nicollet Island, and the North Loop
Old Town Reinvented

Above: *Third Avenue Bridge and Old St. Anthony*

BOUNDARIES: First St. N., Plymouth Ave. N., Main St. NE, Hennepin Ave. E.
HUDSON'S TWIN CITIES STREET ATLAS COORDINATES: Map 394, 2A, 3A, 2B, and 3B
DISTANCE: About 2 miles
DIFFICULTY: Easy
PARKING: Free 4-hour parking on Island Ave. E. and Island Ave. W.
PUBLIC TRANSIT: Bus lines 2, 11, and 17

Minneapolis was born on the shores of the then-murky Mississippi River. Bridge Square and the Gateway District were the original housing and government centers of the hardworking city in the 19th century. In the early years of the Mill City, lumbering was the main source of wealth, and Boom Island was where the branded logs were sorted. The Gateway was then the locus of the city, where Hennepin Avenue and Nicollet Avenue converged, with Bridge Square at the south side of the Hennepin Avenue Bridge. Nicollet Island remained a blighted industrial area until the 1960s, and Basset Creek in the 1850s was the site for at least seven sawmills. Until the 1950s, the area was an industrial warehouse district. In the past few decades, the area has been transformed. First came the arts organizations, restaurants, nightclubs, and coffee shops. Then came the renovated and newly constructed condos, lofts, and townhomes to form the residential North Loop that we see today. Nicollet Island is now a place where nature and beautifully restored Victorian homes exist within walking distance of downtown, while the Gateway and Bridge Square areas have long since been incorporated into downtown's business and residential district.

Walk Description

Begin on Nicollet Island, at the top of the steps where Island Avenue East and Island Avenue West converge. Descend the railroad-tie stairs, turn left, and cross the pedestrian bridge to ❶ **Boom Island Park.** The iron truss bridge was salvaged from the Wisconsin Central Railroads—an industrial advancement that made the park's name a misnomer because the eastern channel is now connected to the mainland.

Turn left at the fork, and at the next two pedestrian intersections, follow the path closest and parallel to the Mississippi River.

Turn left at the boat launch area. Follow the pedestrian bridge across the channel to the steps of the Plymouth Avenue Bridge.

Turn left at the top of the stairs on the Plymouth Avenue Bridge. The bridge provides a scenic vista of downtown to the south and of Nordeast on the east side of the river.

Boom Island miniature lighthouse and former boat launch

The Gateway District and Bridge Square: The Other Old Town Minneapolis

During the early years of Minneapolis, Bridge Square and the neighboring Gateway District were central to the development of the nascent city. Bridge Square was the area located immediately across the Hennepin Avenue Bridge, and adjacent was the Gateway, where Nicollet and Hennepin Avenues converged to form the hub of the developing city. In 1850 Colonel John Stevens built a home—long since relocated to Minnehaha Park—on a site near the current U.S. Post Office building, where Minneapolis and Hennepin County were founded. Here the first of the four bridges spanning the east and west banks of the Mississippi was built in 1855. Goose Pond was contained in Bridge Square early in its history. The pond's location diverted traffic in the direction of the present route of Nicollet Mall, toward Fort Snelling. Shortly after the pond was drained in 1882, a 275-foot-high light tower was constructed to illuminate the city, only to be torn down after 10 years due to system failures. Later the city developed massive projects such as the Great Northern Railroad (1914) and Gateway Park Pavilion (1915) that replaced the original small buildings.

This was the beginning of a long, dramatic end for Bridge Square. The Gateway District became the working-class center of the city, with hundreds of flophouses and bars for the transient population. Eventually the area became a skid row and the pavilion a sad, decaying hobo hangout. In 1957 the city began its downtown revitalization when 17 blocks were leveled. Gateway Park Pavilion was one of numerous historic buildings, some dating back to the 1850s, that were demolished. The area's significance declined in the vastly expanding city—Gateway Park was replaced by enormous uninspired condos, apartments, and office buildings. Bridge Square is now occupied by busy thoroughfares and the Federal Reserve Bank (1997).

Turn left to go south on West River Parkway and follow the center pedestrian path (stay out of the bicycle lane). Across the parkway is the North End neighborhood.

Turn left at the Grand Rounds information kiosk and follow the path downhill toward the river, winding through peaceful urban parkland lined with mature trees and plentiful plant species.

Turn left at the sign for the bridge that crosses Bassett Creek. The creek was named after lumberman Joel Bassett, who in 1852 built a farm and the first steam-powered sawmill in the vicinity. Sadly, for much of the city's history, 1.5 miles of the creek have been diverted into a concrete storm sewer under Minneapolis that runs into the Mississippi River. Additional rustic walking paths are available for exploration of the creek and its surroundings.

Turn left at the end of the bridge, stay on the middle cement sidewalk along the river, and then go immediately left again.

After passing the parking lot on West River Parkway, turn right on Fourth Avenue North to go southwest. Here you'll see a couple of huge condo projects—the gated Landings on the right and Renaissance on the River on the left.

Turn left on First Street North. On the right are a number of striking condo renovations and constructions, such as the Rock Island Lofts.

Continue and cross the bridge. On the right is ❷ **Spoon and Stable,** which offers seasonal Midwestern cuisine with a French twist. On the left is ❸ **Bachelor Farmer,** owned by Governor Mark Dayton's sons; it serves gourmet comfort food with a Scandinavian twist. If you're not careful, you'll walk right past this wonderful, understated restaurant's front door without noticing it. Bachelor Farmer once held an annual *kräftskiva,* (crayfish party) featuring a crayfish boil and local beer and music. The venture proved so successful that clothing retailer Askov Finlayson moved to 204 N. First St., and the building was converted to a café, where the Bachelor Farmer curates food in a fast-casual environment.

A block ahead and on the right is the ❹ **Alliance Française,** which promotes French culture through language classes, lectures, social events, music, and film at various sites throughout the Twin Cities.

Turn left on Hennepin Avenue, where the Federal Reserve Bank—once the locus of Bridge Square—is located. Kitty-corner from the intersection of First Avenue North and Hennepin Avenue is the George Washington Memorial Flagstaff (1917)—the only object that remains, although slightly moved, from the original Gateway Park and the Gateway District.

Continue on the Hennepin Avenue Bridge. Italian horror-film director Dario Argento shot his first American film, *Trauma,* in Minneapolis in 1993. It's on this bridge that the character played by the director's daughter, actress Asia Argento, attempts suicide—with the local landmark, the Grain Belt Beer sign, behind her.

At the end of the bridge, make an immediate left, descend the stairs, and turn right at the bottom of the stairs. On the right is DeLaSalle High School, a Catholic high school on the island since 1900.

Continue straight across Grove Street. To the right are the Eastman Flats (1877), an excellent example of French Second Empire row houses, constructed with local limestone.

Keep straight, crossing the railroad tracks. At the parking lot for ❺ **Nicollet Island Park,** turn right and follow the path through the woods.

Turn left on Nicollet Street and take in the beautiful Victorian homes.

Continue straight on Nicollet Street until it ends, and then follow the paved path through the park and woods to finish the walk.

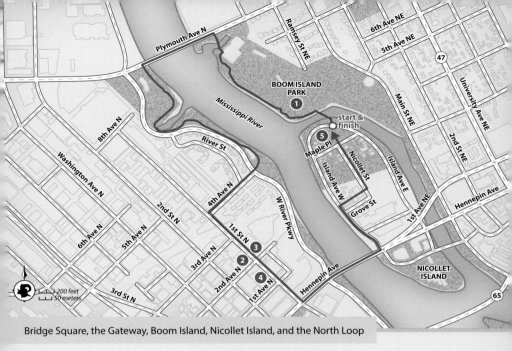

Bridge Square, the Gateway, Boom Island, Nicollet Island, and the North Loop

Points of Interest

1   **Boom Island Park**   minneapolisparks.org, 724 Sibley St. NE, Minneapolis, 612-230-6400

2   **Spoon and Stable,**   spoonandstable.com, 211 First. St. N., Minneapolis, 612-224-9850

3   **The Bachelor Farmer**   thebachelorfarmer.com, 50 N. Second Ave., Minneapolis, 612-206-3920

4   **Alliance Française**   afmsp.org, 113 First St. N., Minneapolis, 612-332-0436

5   **Nicollet Island Park**   minneapolisparks.org, 724 Sibley St. NE, Minneapolis, 612-230-6400

13 Historic Mill District
Industrial Wasteland Renewed as Scenic Urban Playground

Above: The Stone Arch Bridge over the Mississippi River

BOUNDARIES: 11th Ave. S., Second St. S., Hennepin Ave. E., Main St. SE
HUDSON'S TWIN CITIES STREET ATLAS COORDINATES: Map 394, 3B
DISTANCE: About 2.5 miles
DIFFICULTY: Moderate
PARKING: Limited free parking on Second St. and Sixth Ave.; metered parking on Main St.
PUBLIC TRANSIT: Bus lines 2, 4, 7, 17, and 22

The Historic Mill District is not a neighborhood but a confluence of historic Minneapolis communities surrounding the city's quintessential life source: waterpower from St. Anthony Falls. Energy was a limited commodity in the 19th century, and the abundant hydroelectric source provided an accessible, affordable, and consistent supply. As a result, industry, followed by communities, developed on both east and west banks of the energy-rich Mississippi River.

The city of St. Anthony, on the east bank, came into existence in 1838 under the leadership of lumber and milling entrepreneur Franklin Steele. Minneapolis, on the west bank, was not founded until 1852 but flourished after annexing St. Anthony in 1872. The proximity to waterpower and the farms of the Upper Midwest transformed Minneapolis into a world leader in flour production from 1880 to 1920. In this milieu, two giants in the industry—General Mills and Pillsbury—emerged and consolidated the industry, later becoming omnipresent, diversified national brands. However, the milling industry gradually decentralized, and General Mills moved its headquarters to suburban Golden Valley and closed the Washburn A Mill in 1965. The descent began, and the area was largely abandoned until the 1970s. The renovation began in Old St. Anthony, reaching a crescendo with the condo building boom at the beginning of this century. The industrial birthplace of Minneapolis has become one of the city's most beautiful locales—a fact that would no doubt amaze those early pioneers.

Walk Description

Start at the corner of Sixth Avenue Southeast and Main Street Southeast, and follow the sidewalk south toward the Stone Arch Bridge. On the right is ❶ **Father Hennepin Bluff Park,** where in 1680 a Belgian named Louis Hennepin—at the time a captive of the Dakota Indians—was the first European to encounter St. Anthony Falls, named in honor of Hennepin's patron saint, St. Anthony of Padua.

Turn right to cross the Stone Arch Bridge. The bridge was constructed in 1883 by James J. Hill to complete his St. Paul, Minneapolis, and Manitoba Railroad, which later became the Great Northern Railroad. The only stone bridge on the Mississippi, the immense limestone bridge cuts diagonally across the river for 2,100 feet. It remained in operation until 1978 and reopened after renovation as a pedestrian and bicycle bridge in 1994.

At the end of the bridge, immediately turn left and enter ❷ **Mill Ruins Park,** where you can catch a glimpse of the remains of first-generation mills along the river.

To your right are examples of Minneapolis's longtime ties with waterpower. Starting in 1857, the Minneapolis Mill Company, a consortium, controlled and operated the waterpower on the west side of the river, with 25 flour mills and 30 industrial buildings. In 1885 the consortium deepened and lengthened the canal to use as its power source.

Continue descending on the path and turn right. On the left are the ❸ **Upper St. Anthony Falls Lock and Dam,** with an observation area and public restroom.

Turn right and follow the metal staircase across the tailrace. Here, you can read about the area's history and archaeological-dig findings, documented on markers.

Turn left on the metal boardwalk after exploring the mill ruins. At the end of the sidewalk, turn right and go uphill toward the enormous mills and the intersection of 11th Avenue and West River Parkway, passing the I-35W Bridge Remembrance Garden.

After crossing West River Parkway, follow the middle path through **❹ Gold Medal Park.** The park was named after the General Mills flour of the same name, which won the Miller's Exhibition in Cincinnati in 1880 and brought national prominence to the brand.

Turn right on Second Street South, passing the park's large sign. From here, you can see the Guthrie Theater and the Mill City Museum, with downtown in the background. On Second Street, due east, **❺ Izzy's Ice Cream** offers a variety of creations—every single-scoop cone is topped with a tiny second scoop, an "izzy," so you can sample another flavor for free.

Continue northwest, toward Jean Nouvel's internationally acclaimed **❻ Guthrie Theater.** The French architect designed the theater with this site in mind, and it fits in well beside the immense renovated mills. Not only does it include three theaters, but it also has a restaurant, bars, and a cantilever overhanging West River Parkway.

Turn right at the huge picture of British director Sir Tyrone Guthrie, the theater's founder, on the side of the building. On the left is **❼ Spoonriver** restaurant, owned by local culinary legend Brenda

The Mill City Museum, built in the ruins of what was once the world's largest flour mill

Langton. Organic produce and grass-fed meats feature on the delicious menu, which includes weekend brunches. In the shed between the restaurant, the ❽ **Mill City Museum,** and the Guthrie is the ❾ **Mill City Farmers Market,** held on Saturdays, May–October.

The Aster Café and its outdoor dining area

Turn left. On the left is the Washburn A Mill Complex (1880), home of the company that, through mergers, became General Mills. The first Washburn A Mill exploded on May 2, 1878, killing 18 in one of the city's greatest industrial disasters. The second A Mill was vacant for a number of years and caught fire in 1991, destroying much of the roof and walls. In 2003, the ruins were renovated and redesigned by Meyer, Scherer & Rockcastle Ltd. as a multiuse structure that includes the Mill City Museum, restaurants, and condos. The museum, operated by the Minnesota Historical Society, features exhibits and an elevator ride to a rooftop observation deck.

Turn right at the MILL RUINS PARK sign, crossing West River Parkway, and then take a left on the pedestrian path. Turn right, following the riverside pedestrian path, and turn left next to the waterpower headrace. On the left is a series of historic mills, such as the Crown Roller Mill (1878), which was renovated and converted into office space.

Continue northwest under the Third Avenue Bridge. Up ahead is the U.S. Post Office (1934), an enormous three-block Art Deco Mankato Kasota Stone building. Well worth a visit is ❿ **First Bridge Park,** located directly ahead. Here you can stop to read the interpretive information on the four bridges that have occupied the site since it became the first permanent span across the Mississippi River in 1855.

Turn left to go up the first set of stairs, and turn right onto the Hennepin Avenue Bridge.

Turn right on Wilder Street. The Nicollet Island Pavilion and park for St. Anthony Falls are straight ahead—a detour to this scenic spot is well worth it.

Turn left after crossing Merriam Street and continue along it. On the left is the ⓫ **Nicollet Island Inn,** a swanky destination for fine dining, five-course meals, and Sunday brunches, plus elegant lodging in the converted Island Sash and Door Works (1893). Until the middle of the 20th century, Nicollet Island was a vast industrial area packed with factories and not the pristine park it is today.

After crossing the Merriam Street Bridge, turn right on Main Street Southeast. The bridge was salvaged from the Broadway Avenue Bridge upriver to become one of the four spans. On the left is Riverplace, developed in 1984 as a mall and restaurant complex—unfortunately, only restaurants remain in this former urban mall. The ⓬ **Wilde Cafe** serves gourmet comfort food and award-winning desserts in an intimate setting. After passing under the Third Avenue Bridge you'll see ⓭ **St. Anthony Main Theatre** on the left, where the Minneapolis–St. Paul International Film Festival is held every spring. Next door is ⓮ **Pracna** (1890), a restaurant and bar with elegant food and specialty beers. It's also where the rebirth of Old St. Anthony began—Pracna was used first as a residence in 1969 before being converted into a restaurant a few years later. At the end of the block is the ⓯ **Aster Cafe** (1855), a relaxing place to enjoy coffee, sandwiches, soups, and salads in Minneapolis's oldest extant commercial building. ⓰ **Jefe** serves high-quality, midpriced Mexican-inspired food On the right is the most recent addition to Old St. Anthony: ⓱ **Water Power Park,** where walkers have a view above St. Anthony Falls.

Cross Third Avenue Southeast. The enormous, historic Pillsbury A Mill, with limestone walls 8 feet thick in some areas, is in the controversial process of being converted into condos. On the right are stairs leading down to Hennepin Island via the Lower Path—a beautiful piece of nature where you can get a close look at the crumbling brick façades of old factories. Unfortunately, erosion has resulted in the closure of sections of the already-rough trail.

Finish the walk at the intersection of Main Street Southeast and Sixth Avenue Southeast.

Points of Interest

❶ **Father Hennepin Bluff Park/Stone Arch Bridge** minneapolisparks.org, 420 Main St. SE, Minneapolis, 612-230-6400

❷ **Mill Ruins Park** minneapolisparks.org, 103 Portland Ave. S., Minneapolis, 612-230-6400

❸ **Upper St. Anthony Falls Lock and Dam** nps.gov/miss/planyourvisit/uppestan.htm, 1 Portland Ave. S., Minneapolis, 612-333-5336

Historic Mill District

④ **Gold Medal Park** nps.gov/miss/planyourvisit/goldmedal.htm, Second St. S. and 11th Ave. S., Minneapolis, 612-230-6400

⑤ **Izzy's Ice Cream,** izzysicecream.com, 1100 Second St. S., Minneapolis, 612-206-3356

⑥ **Guthrie Theater** guthrietheater.org, 818 Second St. S., Minneapolis, 612-377-2224

⑦ **Spoonriver** spoonriver.com, 750 Second St. S., Minneapolis, 612-436-2236

⑧ **Mill City Museum** millcitymuseum.org, 704 Second St. S., Minneapolis, 612-341-7555

⑨ **Mill City Farmers Market** millcityfarmersmarket.org, 704 Second St. S., Minneapolis, 612-341-7580

⑩ **First Bridge Park** minneapolisparks.org, 1 W. River Pkwy., Minneapolis, 612-230-6400

⑪ **Nicollet Island Inn** nicolletislandinn.com, 95 Merriam St., Minneapolis, 612-331-1800

⑫ **Wilde Cafe** wildecafe.com, 65 Main St. SE, Minneapolis, 612-331-4544

⑬ **St. Anthony Main Theatre** stanthonymaintheatre.com, 115 Main St. SE, Minneapolis, 612-331-4723

⑭ **Pracna** pracna-on-main.business.site, 117 Main St. SE, Minneapolis, 612-379-3200

⑮ **Aster Cafe** astercafe.com, 121 Main St. SE, Minneapolis, 612-379-3138

⑯ **Jefe** jefeminneapolis.com, 219 Main St. SE, Minneapolis, 612-255-2000

⑰ **Water Power Park** minneapolisparks.org, 204 Main St. SE, Minneapolis, 612-230-6400

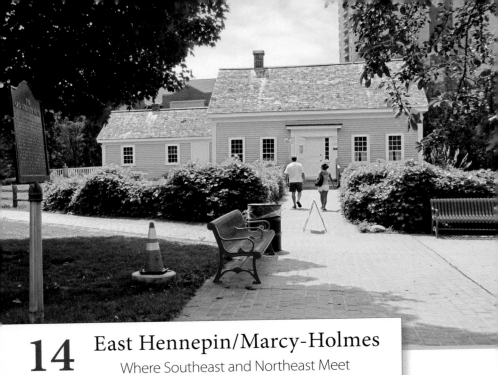

14 East Hennepin/Marcy-Holmes
Where Southeast and Northeast Meet

Above: *The Ard Godfrey House in Chute Square*

BOUNDARIES: Central Ave. SE, Lourdes Pl., First Ave. NE, Seventh St. NE
HUDSON'S TWIN CITIES STREET ATLAS COORDINATES: Map 394, 3A and 3B
DISTANCE: About 1.25 miles
DIFFICULTY: Easy
PARKING: Free parking on Sixth St. SE
PUBLIC TRANSIT: Bus lines 2, 4, and 11

A few decades ago, you would have been hard-pressed to find anyone truly excited about visiting this little area that weaves in and out of both Northeast and Southeast Minneapolis. Today it's a destination for haute couture shopping, drinking, and dining. Previously, this mostly dilapidated historic district was where now-defunct shops such as Cashman's Furniture and Bank's department store struggled to bring in customers. These days, however, the area has been reborn into something of an extension of nearby downtown Minneapolis, with all the glamour and sophistication of the uptown district.

Walk Description

Start at Hennepin Avenue East and Sixth Street Southeast in front of ❶ **Brasa Rotisserie,** owned by Alex Roberts, winner of the James Beard Award for Best Chef in the Midwest. Stop in and try some of its wonderful food, which includes rotisserie chicken and pork shoulder roast, all of which is organically raised on local farms.

Carefully cross Hennepin Avenue East, heading northwest, and go straight to the stop sign by the Holiday gas station. Across the street at 523 Hennepin Ave. E. is the former site of the original Totino's Pizza—that's right, the creators of those thin frozen pizzas and bite-size pizza rolls. After nearly 56 years at this location, the restaurant moved to the cheaper suburbs in 2007 and quickly closed, but a plaque that commemorates the original Totino's restaurant can be found on the new building that occupies the site. Today ❷ **Glam Doll Donuts** can be found here, serving specialty donuts named after local celebrities and musicians, with suggested beer pairings.

Turn right to follow Central Avenue Southeast and go straight (northeast). Across the street is ❸ **The Bad Waitress,** a funky diner with excellent food and Northeast Minneapolis–inspired art.

Turn left to cross Central Avenue and go southwest on First Avenue Northeast. Across the street and to the left is the big Bank's building at 615 First Ave. NE, which was a Sears-like discount store for many years before being converted into an office building.

Cross Sixth Street Northeast and go straight. Across the street is the ❹ **Red Stag Supperclub,** with its distinctive statue of a red stag directly above the sign. The Red Stag shares owners with the upscale Café Barbette and Bryant Lake Bowl & Cabaret Theater; all three restaurants are notable for serving food crafted from sustainable organic farms. To your left are the Melrose Flats, built in the 1890s. Once fairly run-down, they've recently been renovated into snazzy-looking businesses and loft condos. On your right is ❺ **I Like You,** which carries a rotating selection of artwork, jewelry, and clothing made by local artisans.

Turn left on Fifth Street Northeast. This takes you along the redbrick facade of the Melrose Flats buildings. Stop and look at the two rock-and-steel Zoran Mojsilov sculptures along the front of ❻ **Gardens of Salonica,** an elegant Greek restaurant open for lunch and dinner.

Turn right at Hennepin Avenue East to cross Fifth Street Northeast and go west along Hennepin Avenue. Across the street to your left is the former site of the Third Northwestern National Bank, now an empty parking lot. On December 16, 1932, one of the bloodiest bank robberies in Minnesota history took place here. The Barker-Karpis gang—linked to Ma Barker and Alvin "Creepy" Karpis—robbed the bank of more than $12,000, killing two Minneapolis police officers and injuring more in the process.

Cross University Avenue. To your right is ❼ **Kramarczuk's,** a family-run deli and restaurant selling homemade sausages, breads, pastries, and other Eastern European cuisine since 1954. Kramarczuk's also hosts an Easter festival and other seasonal events—all with an Eastern European flavor. Across the street to your left is ❽ **Punch Neopolitan Pizza,** an excellent local chain.

Cross Second Street Southeast and turn left to cross Hennepin Avenue East. Make an immediate right to walk in front of the site of the former Nye's Polonaise Room, once declared by *Esquire* to be *the* best bar in America, and sadly, closed. Two of the four buildings—the former harness shop and tavern—will be renovated within the condominium complex.

Turn left at Lourdes Place. On your left is ❾ **Our Lady of Lourdes Catholic Church,** the city's oldest church. The front part of the church was erected in 1857 for a Universalist congregation but was later sold to a French Catholic group that added the transept, apse, and bell tower in the 1880s. Across the street is the former site of the Industrial Exposition Hall, where the Republican Convention of 1892 nominated incumbent president Benjamin Harrison for a doomed run against Grover Cleveland.

Turn left to follow the brick sidewalk around Our Lady of Lourdes and make an immediate right. Follow the brick path to the corner and cross Bank Street Southeast

Turn left to go northeast. Cross Ortman Street Southeast and take a right to follow the path through ❿ **Chute Square**. To your right is the little yellow ⓫ **Ard Godfrey House,** the oldest existing wood-frame house in Minneapolis. Built in 1848, the house was moved several times before Chute Square became its permanent location. Ard Godfrey's wife, Harriet, is credited for having brought the first dandelions to Minnesota, and The Woman's Club of Minneapolis holds a Dandelion Days festival every summer in her honor.

Cross Central Avenue Southeast and turn left to cross University Avenue Southeast, walking on Central Avenue. On the corner is the former Pillsbury Southeast Library building, now offices for the Phillips Distilling Company. The little building at 326 Central Ave. SE was once Jim's Coffee Shop & Bakery, which was featured in the Christian Slater movie *Untamed Heart*. The amazing building that houses the ⓬ **Aveda Day Spa Institute** on the corner of Central Avenue Southeast and Fourth Street Southeast is the former Cataract Temple, the first Masonic lodge in Minneapolis.

Turn right to walk northeast along Hennepin Avenue East. Up ahead is Brasa Rotisserie, where you started.

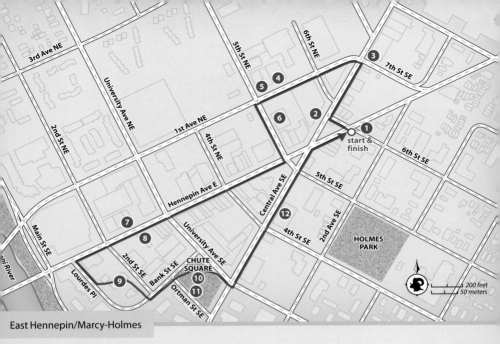

East Hennepin/Marcy-Holmes

Points of Interest

① **Brasa Rotisserie** brasa.us, 600 Hennepin Ave. E., Minneapolis, 612-379-3030

② **Glam Doll Donuts** glamdolldonuts.com, 519 Central Ave. NE, Minneapolis, 612-223-8071

③ **The Bad Waitress** thebadwaitress.com, 700 Central Ave. NE, Minneapolis, 612-354-7947

④ **Red Stag Supperclub** redstagsupperclub.com, 509 Sixth St. NE, Minneapolis, 612-767-7766

⑤ **I Like You** ilikeyouonline.com, 501 First Ave. NE, Minneapolis, 612-208-0249

⑥ **Gardens of Salonica** gardensofsalonica.com, 19 Fifth St. NE, Minneapolis, 612-378-0611

⑦ **Kramarczuk's** kramarczuk.com, 215 Hennepin Ave. E., Minneapolis, 612-379-3018

⑧ **Punch Neopolitan Pizza** punchpizza.com, 210 Hennepin Ave. E., Minneapolis, 612-623-8114

⑨ **Our Lady of Lourdes Catholic Church** ourladyoflourdesmn.com, 1 Lourdes Pl., Minneapolis, 612-379-2259

⑩ **Chute Square** minneapolisparks.org, 28 University Ave. SE, Minneapolis, 612-230-6400

⑪ **Ard Godfrey House** minneapolisparks.org, 28 University Ave. SE, Minneapolis, 612-870-8001

⑫ **Aveda Day Spa Institute** aveda.edu/minneapolis, 400 Central Ave. SE, Minneapolis, 612-331-1400

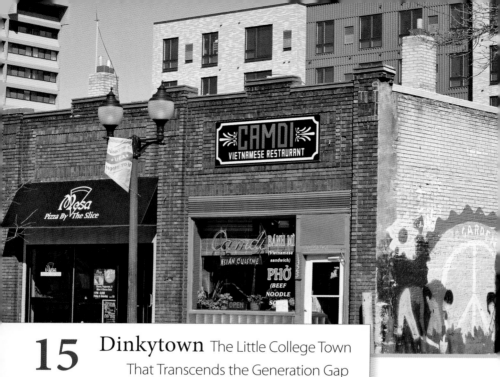

15   Dinkytown The Little College Town That Transcends the Generation Gap

Above: Camdi Vietnamese Restaurant in the Dinkytown Historic District

BOUNDARIES: University Ave. SE, 13th Ave. SE, Fifth St. SE, 15th Ave. SE
HUDSON'S TWIN CITIES STREET ATLAS COORDINATES: Map 394, 4B
DISTANCE: About 0.5 mile
DIFFICULTY: Easy
PARKING: Metered parking on 14th Ave. SE, Fifth St. SE, and Fourth St. SE
PUBLIC TRANSIT: Bus lines 2, 3, and 6

There is a never-ending debate over the origin of the name Dinkytown. The most compelling theories hark back either to the small cars, called dinkies, that hauled railroad goods and workers or to the long-lost "dinky" movie theater. The approximately five-block commercial district of the Marcy–Holmes neighborhood, nestled just north of the University of Minnesota (U of M) campus, is home to nearly 40 restaurants, numerous live-music venues, and plenty of quirky places to shop. To survive here, businesses must cater to the varied tastes of college students (both American and international) and professors in their search for authenticity, value, and adventure. Dinkytown is the Twin Cities' tiny answer to Greenwich Village. In 2015, the heart of Dinkytown was designated as a historic district, in response to homes and institutional buildings being converted into multistory student apartments.

Walk Description

Start at the southeast corner of Fifth Street Southeast and 14th Avenue Southeast, and walk southwest. The Subway parking lot was one of the former haunts of Robert Zimmerman, who later changed his name to Bob Dylan. From his freshman year at the U of M in 1959 until he left for quick fame in New York City in 1961, Dylan performed on the window stage at the tiny coffee shop formerly located on this site, the 10 O'Clock Scholar.

Turn left at the corner of Fourth Street Southeast. ❶ **Himalayan Restaurant** serves fast-casual Indian, Nepali, and Tibetan standards, available at various price points for the college crowd.

Turn right on 15th Street Southeast, and then take an immediate right to continue along Fourth Street Southeast in the opposite direction. From the railing at the intersection, you get an expansive view of Dinkytown, as well as the distant historic Mill District and downtown. Just below the railing, you can see that Dinkytown was constructed about a story above the solitary train track below, an area once clogged with rails leading to downtown Minneapolis.

After crossing 14th Avenue, turn left to go southwest. On the right is ❷ **Loring Bar & Restaurant,** with its stylish and urbane exterior. Glass windows above the entrance are emblazoned with the word *drugs,* a tribute to Gray's Campus Drugs, which occupied this spot for decades before the restaurant and bar opened in 1999.

Just ahead on the right is the ❸ **Kitty Cat Klub**, with the same name as the Berlin nightclub during the interwar period preceding World War II. It is another ultracool spot with drinks, food, and, above all, a hip atmosphere and a back patio. Next door and upstairs, with another marvelous patio vista, is ❹ **Annie's Parlour**, which has served burgers, fries, and malts to several generations of college students.

Turn right on University Avenue Southeast. On the right is the newest location of the ❺ **Purple Onion Café.** The name is a tip of the hat to a coffee shop of the same name during Dylan's brief time in Dinkytown. It moved here after more than a decade at the corner of Fourth Street and 14th Avenue and now offers sandwiches, salads, and an expanded menu.

Bob Dylan: The Ghost of Dinkytown

Bob Dylan—née Robert Zimmerman—is a local specter. Dinkytown became his home in 1959 when he arrived from the iron range town of Hibbing, Minnesota, to study at the University of Minnesota. In the company of baby boomers and Dylan fanatics, grand proclamations are made about arguably the greatest songwriter of the modern era. He is the favorite son whose legacy is omnipresent, thanks to the unbelievable success he attained almost immediately after leaving for New York City in January 1961. In 2016, he was awarded the Nobel Prize in Literature—a long way from his folk singing roots.

The Dinkytown folk scene of this period knew a different version of Dylan than the conquering-hero myth that arose in the ensuing years. Dylan is remembered for being booed off the stage at the tiny 10 O'Clock Scholar during its folk heyday and for purloining rare folk records from contemporaries in the small scene.

Whether Dylan's success was due entirely to talent and ambition or to the desire of his record company, the media, and a growing youth culture to anoint a rough-hewn poet for their generation is debatable. Regardless, Dylan is an international icon who began his career in Dinkytown, and his shadow is cast on everyone and everything in this little neighborhood.

Turn right on 13th Avenue Southeast. Across the street is the **6 Southeast Community Library**, formerly the State Capitol Credit Union. The small modernist building was designed in 1964 by U of M architecture professor Ralph Rapson, who died in 2008. On the corner is a "Positively 4th Street" mural, a song that everyone knows was written about Dinkytown and not New York City—at least here, anyway.

Turn right on Fourth Street Southeast. On the right is the marquee of the **7 Varsity Theater.** The old movie theater, long mothballed, was transformed by the owner of Loring Pasta Bar (recently rebranded as the LRx Loring & Pharmacy Bar) into one of the area's premier concert venues. The theater is now furnished with couches and other comfy accommodations for lounging and enjoying live music. Across the street is **8 Camdi Restaurant,** which serves homey Chinese and Vietnamese food, with plenty of vegetarian and vegan options, at college-friendly prices.

Turn left on 14th Avenue Southeast. This side of the block illustrates the diversity of culinary bounty in Dinkytown. The tiny and legendary **9 Al's Breakfast** serves perfect pancakes, omelets, and eggs Benedict. Just down the block is **10 Wally's,** which serves good, cheap Middle Eastern food—be sure to try the chicken shawarma. Finally, next door, **11 Kafé 421** serves fine cuisine at all price ranges, from its student-priced gyros to its superb steaks and bouillabaisse. Continue northeast on 14th Avenue Southeast to Fifth Street Southeast to finish the walk.

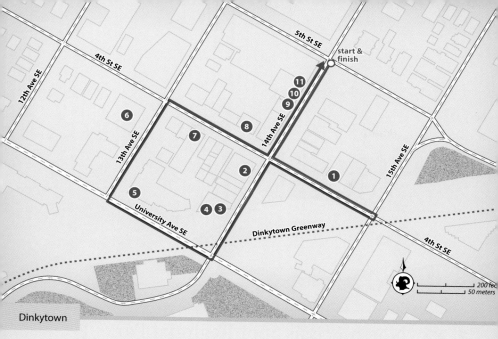

Points of Interest

① **Himalayan Restaurant** himalayanmomo.com, 1415 Fourth St. SE, Minneapolis, 612-332-2910

② **Loring Bar & Restaurant** loringbarrestaurant.com, 327 14th Ave. SE, Minneapolis, 612-378-4849

③ **Kitty Cat Klub** kittycatklub.net, 315 14th Ave. SE, Minneapolis, 612-331-9800

④ **Annie's Parlour** facebook.com/dinkytownannies, 313 14th Ave. SE, Minneapolis, 612-379-0744

⑤ **Purple Onion Café** thepurpleonioncafe.com, 1301 University Ave. SE, Minneapolis, 612-252-0217

⑥ **Southeast Community Library** hclib.org, 1222 Fourth St. SE, Minneapolis, 612-543-6725

⑦ **Varsity Theater** varsitytheater.org, 1308 Fourth St. SE, Minneapolis, 612-604-0222

⑧ **Camdi Restaurant** camdirestaurant.com, 1325 Fourth St. SE, Minneapolis, 612-331-4194

⑨ **Al's Breakfast** alsbreakfastmpls.com, 413 14th Ave. SE, Minneapolis, 612-331-9991

⑩ **Wally's** wallysfalafelandhummus.com, 417 14th Ave. SE, Minneapolis, 612-746-4776

⑪ **Kafé 421** kafe421.com, 421 14th Ave. SE, Minneapolis, 612-623-4900

16 North Mississippi Regional Park and Webber Park

Above: *View of downtown Minneapolis from Camden Bridge*

BOUNDARIES: 37th Ave. NE., Webber Pkwy., 45th Ave. N., Marshall St. NE
HUDSON'S TWIN CITIES STREET ATLAS COORDINATES: Map 367, 1C and 2C
DISTANCE: 1.25 miles
DIFFICULTY: Moderate
PARKING: Free parking on St. Anthony Pkwy.
PUBLIC TRANSIT: Bus line 5

Northeast Minneapolis and ❶ **North Mississippi Regional Park** intersect at the Mississippi River. The plat on both sides of the river was unevenly sewn together where 37th Avenue Northeast crosses to become 42nd Avenue Northwest. Extending from I-94 and the river north to the I-694 interchange, the park is operated by the Minneapolis Park and Recreation Board up to 57th Avenue North, and by the Three Rivers Park District north of that. This walk traverses the southern section. Once brickyards, quarries, the city workhouse, and public housing (Hopewell Hospital, the sanatorium for tuberculosis patients, and the Mississippi Courts Apartments), the area is now an urban nature oasis.

This unique walk through nature is bisected by I-94, the Canadian Pacific Railroad, and the Soo Line Bridge (1905), approximately 0.25 mile due southeast, with the Camden Bridge affording a spectacular view of the Mississippi River and downtown Minneapolis.

If you like, you can extend the walk to include Webber Park (formerly Camden Park), renamed for Charles C. and Mary Webber in 1939, who paid for the public baths once located there.

Walk Description

Start at the combined pedestrian/bike path. Carefully follow the path as it wends under the Camden Bridge, and note the wildlife, birds, and fish in a distinctly urban setting.

Continue on the path up the hill. Take a right at the kiosk, and then turn right at the stop sign and walk onto the bridge. Enjoy the view of the Mississippi River.

Midway across the bridge, descend the stairs or the ramp to the park. Seasonally, birds serenade listeners under the bridge deck—and if you're lucky, you'll encounter a bird imitating a car alarm.

At the bottom of the stairs, follow the winding path down. At the bottom of the hill, cross the bridge. Continue straight, or turn right and walk down to the river.

After crossing the bridge across Shingle Creek, follow the path closest to the creek. For further nature exploration, feel free to travel up the hill, and then return to the walk.

After passing the bridge over the creek, continue on the path under I-94, and follow the path along the creek under the Lyndale Avenue Bridge.

Follow the path across the creek, passing the man-made waterfall. Follow the path up the hill and take a left, or, for further exploration, walk straight ahead to ❷ Webber Park and the Webber Park Natural Swimming Pool. The pool was the first in North America to filter water with plants and microbes rather than chemicals.

Where the pedestrian/bike path merges, turn right on Lyndale Avenue North, crossing Webber Parkway.

Cross 42nd Street and turn left, then walk over I-94, railroad tracks, and an industrial zone. Then, at the steps, explore the park before returning to the route. After returning to the route, observe the view due south of downtown Minneapolis.

Take a right at the end of the bridge and follow the sidewalk to the pedestrian/bike path to finish the walk.

North Mississippi Regional Park and Webber Park

Points of Interest

1. **North Mississippi Regional Park** minneapolisparks.org, 5114 Lyndale Ave. N., Minneapolis, 612-370-4865

2. **Webber Park** minneapolisparks.org, 4400 Dupont Ave. N., Minneapolis, 612-370-4916

17   U of M Public-Land-Grant University in the Shadow of Downtown

BOUNDARIES: Washington Ave. SE, W. River Pkwy., Fourth St. SE, Oak St. SE
HUDSON'S TWIN CITIES STREET ATLAS COORDINATES: Map 394, 4B and 4C
DISTANCE: About 2.5 miles
DIFFICULTY: Easy
PARKING: 2-hour parking on Oak St.; municipal parking lot on the south side of Oak St.
PUBLIC TRANSIT: Numerous bus lines to U of M; light rail

The University of Minnesota is the primary postsecondary institution in the state for education and research. Almost everyone in the region has had some contact with the U of M—often simply referred to as The U—as a student or with Golden Gopher sports. The U is a comprehensive public-land-grant university with a national and international reputation in diverse academic disciplines. Esteemed alumni include late journalist Eric Sevareid; Harry Reasoner of *60 Minutes;* Earl Bakken, inventor of the pacemaker; and Norman Borlaug, the father of the

Green Revolution in agriculture. National Baseball Hall of Fame members Dave Winfield and Paul Molitor also attended the U of M, as did Bob Dylan. Another influential dropout was Hubert H. Humphrey, the 1968 Democratic presidential nominee. The architecture, though, is not as outstanding as the school's most successful graduates. Architectural inspiration is often trumped by functionality; still, there are several noteworthy buildings in scenic settings near the Mississippi River. Thrifty and competitive dining options fit the needs of college students in nearby Stadium Village.

Walk Description

Start at the northwest corner of Oak Street Southeast and Washington Avenue Southeast, and walk west on the sidewalk beside the colossal copper-covered, geodic **❶ McNamara Alumni Center.** The center is at the back of the block and serves as a "front door" to The U. Inside is the Heritage Gallery, honoring the accomplishments of students, alumni, and faculty, with the Memorial Stadium Archway as its centerpiece.

Continue through Stadium Village, the small commercial district next to the former location of Memorial Stadium, where the Minnesota Golden Gophers football team played from 1924 to 1981. **❷ Afro Deli** serves delicious Somali/Middle Eastern rice bowls, sandwiches, wraps, *sambusas,* and Chicken Fantastic. On the left, after crossing Harvard Street Southeast, you'll see the Phillips-Wangensteen Building and Malcolm Moos Health Science Tower—rather uninviting and hulking 1970s brutalist architecture for the world-renowned **❸ University of Minnesota** medical campus.

Turn right, following the sidewalk to the base of the bridge, where the path veers left in front of Ford Hall. Turn left to cross the bridge to enjoy the fine view of downtown and the Mississippi River on the right. Turn left at the end of the bridge, then turn right in front of the recently renovated Coffman Union.

Veer right on the sidewalk, passing the reflective stainless steel of the **❹ Weisman Art Museum,** completed in 1993. It was one of the first art museums designed by deconstructivist architect Frank Gehry. The University of Minnesota president at the time, Nils Hasselmo, instructed the architect, "Don't build another brick lump." Gehry succeeded by creating a local icon with provocative exterior architecture that has polarized opinions, especially with its trademark geometric shapes and mishmash facade facing the Mississippi River. Inside, the Weisman has many outstanding galleries.

Turn left on the pedestrian path atop the Washington Avenue Bridge as it crosses the river. From this bridge, poet and U of M English professor John Berryman committed suicide by jumping to his death on a frigid January day in 1972.

Turn right at the end of the bridge and right again to reverse direction. The West Bank of The U opened in the early 1960s to accommodate the burgeoning student population and has continually expanded. The architecture is functional but relatively uninspiring. The buildings are tied together by a vast network of underground paths. This is a brilliant adaptation, considering the often-inclement weather. It also creates the inaccurate impression aboveground that the area is a ghost town for much of the year.

Below the bridge and slightly upriver on the West Bank is the ⑤ **Bohemian Flats Park,** site of the former Bohemian Flats. First settled in the late 19th century, Bohemian Flats had 1,200 residents in the then–heavily polluted industrial area in 1900. Until 1963, a few homes still remained in this poor, pan-Slavic immigrant neighborhood. After the tragic collapse of the I-35W Bridge on August 1, 2007, the area served as a salvage area and later as a staging area for the cleanup and reconstruction of the new bridge. Now it's a scenic prairie grass–filled piece of parkland and a boat launch for Padelford Riverboats. Much of the public park is now used as a parking lot for boat passengers.

At the end of the bridge, follow the middle pedestrian path above Washington Avenue east toward Northrop Mall, then turn left, passing Kolthoff Hall, and turn right at the end of the building. In 1908, nationally acclaimed local architect Cass Gilbert won a university competition to design future buildings and the mall. Of course, in the battle between artistic vision and economics, the latter won out, and his plan was severely compromised over the years. The mall did not reach the Mississippi River as planned, and the buildings were constructed of brick rather than stone. The results are functional institutional buildings constructed long after Gilbert had moved on to larger designs.

Turn left on the mall at the building on the corner. On the left, almost at the end of the mall, is the Walter Library, renovated in 2001.

Walk up the stairs in front of the Northrop Auditorium, and then turn left to go down the stairs as the sidewalk angles right.

Turn right on Pleasant Street Southeast. The street is filled with numerous long-standing campus buildings—some, such as Nicholson Hall, have been renovated within the past decade.

Turn left on Pillsbury Drive Southeast. On the corner is Eddy Hall. Constructed in 1886 by legendary local architect LeRoy Buffington, it's the oldest standing building on campus. Ahead on the left is Burton Hall, another design by Buffington in the Greek Revival style with a Doric portico and columns. Across the street is a bronze sculpture (1900) by U of M Board of Regents member Daniel French and Governor John Pillsbury, one of the great early supporters of the fledgling university.

On the left in front of Shevlin Hall is a stone marking Old Main. Constructed in 1856, it was lost in a 1904 fire. Old Main was the first building at The U after moving from its original location near Chute Square, where it began as a preparatory school in Old St. Anthony.

Turn right on East River Parkway, passing the dull, institutional Peik Hall on the right.

Turn right on University Avenue Southeast, following the wrought iron fence. After crossing Pleasant Street Southeast you'll see on the right the Tudor and Jacobean architecture of Folwell Hall, with its extensive terra-cotta trim around the doors, windows, and roof. The building is named in honor of William Watts Folwell, the school's first president (1869–1884) and author of *A History of Minnesota,* a superb four-volume early history of the state.

Continue southeast on University Avenue Southeast. Ahead on the left is the vast majority of the Greek Letter Chapter House Historic District. Between 17th Avenue Southeast and Williams Arena is the greatest concentration of period-revival architecture.

Turn left at the pedestrian crosswalk before ❻ **Williams Arena,** when you see Cooke Hall on the right. It was from here to Oak Street Southeast that Memorial Stadium once stood and where the Minnesota Golden Gophers won six national championships—unfortunately they won none after 1960, and they moved to the Hubert H. Humphrey Metrodome in 1982.

Turn right on Fourth Street Southeast and follow the north side of Williams Arena. Since 1928, "the barn" has hosted countless athletic events—primarily home games of the Gophers men's basketball team. The classic brown-brick exterior is surpassed only by the interior, which still makes for great sports-watching, with its excellent sight lines and lively collegiate atmosphere.

TCF Stadium, home of the Golden Gophers

Continue south, following the contour of Oak Street Southeast as it bends across from the new TCF Bank Stadium.

Continue following Oak Street Southeast to Washington Avenue Southeast to finish the walk. Across the street is ❼ **Stub & Herb's** bar and restaurant, one of the best places in the Twin Cities for Summit, Surly, and Schell's, as well as other local and national microbrews on tap, and Minnesota Golden Gophers football.

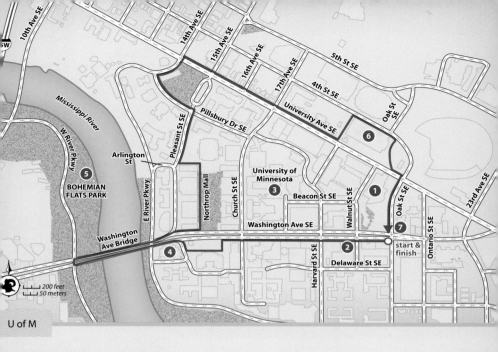

Points of Interest

1. **McNamara Alumni Center** mac-events.org, 200 Oak St. SE, Minneapolis, 612-624-9831

2. **Afro Deli** afrodeli.com, 720 Washington Ave. SE, Minneapolis, 612-871-5555

3. **University of Minnesota** umn.edu/twincities, 100 Church St. SE, Minneapolis, 612-625-2008

4. **Weisman Art Museum** weisman.umn.edu, 333 E. River Pkwy., Minneapolis, 612-625-9494

5. **Bohemian Flats Park** minneapolisparks.org, 2200 W. River Pkwy., Minneapolis, 612-230-6400

6. **Williams Arena** gophersports.com/facilities, 1925 University Ave. SE, Minneapolis, 612-624-3514

7. **Stub & Herb's** stubandherbsbar.com, 227 Oak St. SE, Minneapolis, 612-379-1880

18 Nordeast Minneapolis
Art, Churches, and Bars

Above: *13th Avenue Northeast street scene*

BOUNDARIES: Broadway St. NE, Marshall St. NE, Lowry Ave. NE, Fourth St. NE
HUDSON'S TWIN CITIES STREET ATLAS COORDINATES: Map 394, 2A and 3A; Map 367, 2D and 3D
DISTANCE: About 3.5 miles
DIFFICULTY: Easy
PARKING: Free 2-hour parking on Marshall St. NE and 13th Ave. NE
PUBLIC TRANSIT: Bus lines 6, 11, and 32

For most of Nordeast's history, the neighborhood was strictly blue-collar, where workers from the nearby Gluek Brewing Company and Minneapolis Brewing Company (later Grain Belt), the rail yards, and the casket and furniture factories made their homes. Many of the original houses were built by the occupants—skilled masons and carpenters—and the houses still standing attest to their skills.

Since the 1990s, Nordeast has become younger and hipper as artists, writers, and musicians from the Uptown and Warehouse neighborhoods have found themselves priced out of their apartments. Coffee shops, art galleries, and even condos have replaced many of the old neighborhood bars and repair shops; the bars that have managed to stay open through the renaissance have done so by booking local bands and introducing karaoke. Since the mid-1990s, the neighborhood has held the annual Art-a-Whirl gallery tour every May, one of the largest open studio tours in the country—and one more indication that this neighborhood has changed since its early days.

Walk Description

Start on the corner of 13th Avenue Northeast and Marshall Street Northeast. Facing Grain Belt Brewery/Pierre Bottineau Library, turn right to walk down the left side of Marshall Street Northeast.

Follow the sidewalk north. Across the street is the ❶ **Food Building,** home of the Red Table Meat Co. and Baker's Field Flour and Bread Co. Around the corner is ❷ **The Draft Horse** restaurant, which uses the meat and flour from the adjoining businesses in their potpies, sandwiches, and charcuterie.

Cross the train tracks. To your left, catch a glimpse of the Mississippi River just past the treeline. The deceptively nondescript exterior of ❸ **Psycho Suzi's Motor Lounge** hides the fact that there are three tropical-themed tiki bars inside and a riverside patio.

The tiny ❹ **Gluek Park** reopened in 2007 after undergoing a massive asbestos cleanup. The park gets its name from local brewery Gluek (pronounced "glick," in case you want to order one), and you'll see the company's name painted on old warehouse buildings and bars all over town. ❺ **The Sample Room** serves sample plates of cheese, vegetables, and meats, as well as full-size entrées.

Continue straight, passing the sign for ❻ **Edgewater Park.** If you'd like to take a break, follow the path into the park. This isn't the prettiest look at the Mississippi River, but the views from this vantage point—which include a scrap-metal recycling center and load-bearing barges passing by—give a good picture of the working-class roots of Minneapolis.

Turn right at Lowry Avenue Northeast. ❼ **Betty Danger's Country Club**—featured on the Travel Channel in the summer of 2017—with its impossible-to-miss Ferris wheel, is straight ahead, serving bar food and drinks.

Go east along Lowry Avenue Northeast, all the way to the train tracks. To the right are the downtown Minneapolis skyline, old silos, and warehouse buildings.

Turn right at University Avenue Northeast. **❽ Gasthof Zur Gemütlichkeit** serves a wide selection of tap beers in frighteningly huge boot-shaped glasses. The Gasthof also hosts a popular Oktoberfest in its parking lot, with German food and live music to accompany the copious quantities of beer served. Downstairs is Mario's Keller Bar, which has live music most nights.

Before crossing 22nd Avenue Northeast and continuing south you reach **❾ Bark and the Bite,** an excellent takeout barbecue joint with Southern-style sides, located inside Sunny's Market & Deli. On the corner of 20th Avenue Northeast is **❿ Jax Cafe,** which is the only restaurant in northeast Minneapolis to feature a trout stream running through it. For the past 75 years, this has been a favorite dining spot for people of all ages; around prom time you'll find the place packed with young couples in formal wear. The elegant Kozlak-Radulovich Funeral Chapel, at 1918 University Ave. NE, has been operating here since 1908; it's one of the last reminders that Minneapolis used to be one of the largest coffin producers in the country.

Cross 17th Avenue Northeast and turn left to cross University Avenue Northeast. **⓫ Holy Cross Catholic Church** offers a daily Mass in English and a Sunday Mass in Polish.

View of the former Grain Belt Brewery from northeast Minneapolis

Betty Danger's Country Club with its iconic Ferris wheel

Turn right at Fourth Street Northeast and go south. Pope John Paul II Catholic School (formerly Church of the Holy Cross Catholic School) is on your right.

Turn right at the corner at 13th Avenue Northeast. Nicholas Harper's ⑫ **Rogue Buddha Gallery** is one of the best art galleries in the Twin Cities. The ⑬ **Ritz Theater** originally opened in 1928 but was closed for decades before reopening in 2006 as a performance and event venue. In 2016, Theater Latté Da, a musical theater company, moved in and renovated the building for live productions.

After crossing University Avenue, enjoy the view of ⑭ **SS. Cyril & Methodius Catholic Church,** two blocks ahead at 1301 Second St. NE, with its gorgeous stained glass windows and oxidized copper cupola. On the way is ⑮ **Eat My Words** bookstore, which carries more than 20,000 new and used titles, especially featuring books and events from local writers. On the corner of 13th Avenue Northeast and Second Street is ⑯ **Dangerous Man Brewing Co.,** a taproom in the old Northeast Bank Building that has, in the spirit of Nordeast Minneapolis, repurposed the building into something great, with a dizzying array of the best beers in varying styles, including seemingly discordant yet fantastic flavors such as Peanut Butter Porter and Chocolate Milk

Stout. Next door is **⑰ Young Joni,** serving gourmet pizzas, salads, and cocktails. It's also the only place—other than the taproom—that serves Dangerous Man beer.

Go south on Second Street Northeast and then right at 12th Avenue Northeast. The gigantic, ornate building straight ahead is the former Grain Belt Brewery ("the friendly beer with the friendly flavor"), located at Marshall Street Northeast and 13th Avenue Northeast. The massive, ornately detailed brewery, which was built in 1891, is now home to many local architectural firms, plus a few exclusive galleries.

Cross Main Street Northeast and take the sidewalk to the left. Turn right to go west along Broadway Street Northeast.

Cross the street at Marshall Street Northeast. This takes you past the **⑱ Pierre Bottineau Library,** established in 2001 and built into the Grain Belt Brewery.

Cross the tracks and take a right to carefully follow the still-active train tracks. This takes you along the back side of the Grain Belt Brewery building and the nearby former **⑲ Bottling House,** home of local award-winning publisher Coffee House Press. The buildings are made out of yellow brick and echo the lavish Victorian era of their construction.

Turn right at 13th Avenue Northeast. Straight ahead is the corner of Marshall Street Northeast and 13th Avenue Northeast, our starting point.

Points of Interest

① **Food Building** foodbuilding.com, 1401 Marshall St. NE, Minneapolis, 612-545-5555

② **The Draft Horse** thedrafthorsempls.com, 117 14th Ave. NE, Minneapolis, 612-208-1476

③ **Psycho Suzi's Motor Lounge** psychosuzis.com, 1900 Marshall St. NE, Minneapolis, 612-788-9069

④ **Gluek Park** minneapolisparks.org, 2000 Marshall St. NE, Minneapolis, 612-230-6400

⑤ **The Sample Room** the-sample-room.com, 2124 Marshall St. NE, Minneapolis, 612-789-0333

⑥ **Edgewater Park** minneapolisparks.org, 2326 Marshall St. NE, Minneapolis, 612-230-6400

⑦ **Betty Danger's Country Club** bettydangers.com, 2501 Marshall St. NE, Minneapolis, 612-315-4997

⑧ **Gasthof Zur Gemütlichkeit/Mario's Keller Bar** gasthofzg.com, 2300 University Ave. NE, Minneapolis, 612-781-3860

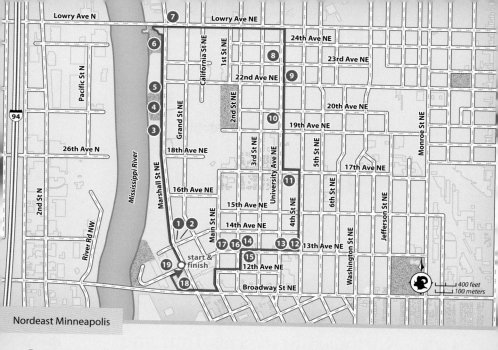

Nordeast Minneapolis

9 **Bark and the Bite at Sunny's Market & Deli** barkandthebite.com, 2207 University Ave. NE, Minneapolis, 612-470-2275

10 **Jax Cafe** jaxcafe.com, 1928 University Ave. NE, Minneapolis, 612-789-7297

11 **Holy Cross Catholic Church** ourholycross.org, 1621 University Ave. NE, Minneapolis, 612-789-7238

12 **Rogue Buddha Gallery** roguebuddha.com, 357 13th Ave. NE, Minneapolis, 612-331-3889

13 **Ritz Theater** ritz-theater.com, 345 13th Ave. NE, Minneapolis, 612-339-3003

14 **SS. Cyril & Methodius Catholic Church** archspm.org, 1315 Second St. NE, Minneapolis, 612-379-9736

15 **Eat My Words** eatmywordsbooks.com, 1228 Second St. NE, Minneapolis, 651-243-1756

16 **Dangerous Man Brewing Co.** dangerousmanbrewing.com, 1300 Second St. NE, Minneapolis, 612-236-4087

17 **Young Joni** youngjoni.com, 165 13th Ave. NE, Minneapolis, 612-345-5719

18 **Pierre Bottineau Library** hclib.org, 55 Broadway St. NE, Minneapolis, 612-630-6890

19 **Grain Belt Bottling House and Warehouse** artspace.org/our-places/grain-belt-studios, 77 and 79 13th Ave. NE, Minneapolis, 612-465-0233

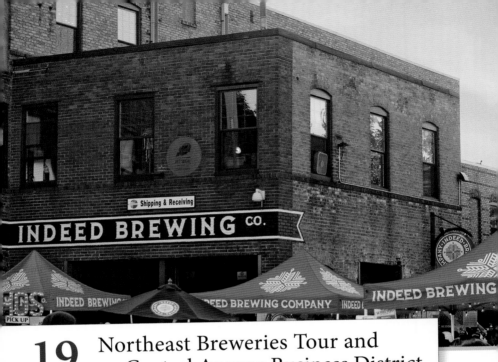

19 Northeast Breweries Tour and Central Avenue Business District

Above: Indeed Brewing Company during Art-a-Whirl

BOUNDARIES: Broadway St. NE, Quincy St. NE, 26th St. NE, Polk St. NE
HUDSON'S TWIN CITIES STREET ATLAS COORDINATES: Map 394, A3 and A4; Map 367, 3D
DISTANCE: 3.25 miles
DIFFICULTY: Moderate
PARKING: Free parking available on Fillmore, Summer, and Polk Sts.
PUBLIC TRANSIT: Bus lines 10 and 17

In Northeast Minneapolis, a continuous skein of artisanship links the past and the present. The heart of the city's then-small Italian-American community, Beltrami Park (formerly Maple Hill Cemetery from 1857 until 1890), was renamed for explorer Giacomo Beltrami, who searched for the Mississippi River's source in 1823. Despite external threats (the construction of I-35W, the failed effort to develop I-335, and successfully navigated urban renewal), the neighborhood survived. It's now the gateway to the Northeast Minneapolis Brewing District, thanks to the Surly Bill (2011). So far, five taprooms alone have sprung up in the immediate neighborhood, if you include the nearby Fair State Brewing Cooperative in the Central Avenue Business District.

Central Avenue, formerly New Boston, was and is Northeast Minneapolis' shopping and dining corridor. Polish, Swedish, and Eastern European businesses once flourished here, but over the past few decades they have been replaced by immigrants from the Middle East, Mexico, Ecuador, and elsewhere. The diversity can be found in eclectic restaurants and ethnic grocery stores.

Walk Description

Start at the corner of Summer and Fillmore Streets and head north. Northeast Minneapolis was constructed before city zoning laws, so factories and renovated industrial buildings sit beside residential homes. Churches such as Our Lady of Mount Carmel Catholic Church were once the center of a thriving Italian community at Beltrami Park.

Cross Broadway Street Northeast and turn left, heading west.

Continue east and cross Tyler Street. On the right is the Broadway Building—grab a coffee at Spyhouse Coffee Company or a beer at 612 Brew on the street level.

Continue east, crossing Central Avenue, with a beautiful view of the business district to the north. The latest Broadway–Central Bridge was constructed in 1987 and reflects the area's rich ethnic history with motifs that include French, Polish, Lebanese, and African.

Turn right on Quincy Street. The large building was renovated into the Highlight Center. It was once the Mazda lightbulb factory, and later, the Minneapolis Public Schools headquarters. On the block in a freestanding structure is Able Seedhouse & Brewery—an example of the new businesses found in the area. It is the first in the state to malt its own barley for brewing. Numerous galleries and diverse businesses line the street. After the sidewalk ends, walk carefully on the east side of the street.

Turn right on 14th Avenue Northeast. North is ❶ **Indeed Brewing Company,** located in the Solar Arts Building. Across the railroad tracks is the immense Northrup King Building, once a huge warehouse that provided seeds to farmers. For several decades, it has housed various art studio galleries.

Turn left to go north on Central Avenue. After passing under the railroad bridge, on the left is the Thorp Building, another massive complex of galleries, businesses, coffee shops, and even ❷ **Tattersall Distilling's** craft cocktail lounge.

Continue straight, crossing 18½ Avenue. On the left is ❸ **Maya Cuisine,** frequently lauded as one of the best Mexican restaurants in the Twin Cities.

On the left after you cross 22nd Avenue is the Northeast Library. Inside, near the computers, images of the history of the neighborhood, once known as New Boston, are displayed on matte backgrounds.

Continuing north, after crossing 24th Avenue, you encounter several outstanding dining options: ❹ **El Taco Riendo,** specializing in savory tacos; ❺ **Costa Blanca Bistro,** featuring critically acclaimed tapas; and ❻ **Sen Yai Sen Lek,** offering fresh Thai food.

After crossing Lowry Avenue, on the left is ❼ **Fair State Brewing Cooperative.** Next door is ❽ **Aki's BreadHaus,** with authentic German bread and pastries.

Turn right to cross 26th Avenue, and then turn right again to head south on Central Avenue. Ahead is ❾ **Holy Land**—a bakery, grocery, restaurant, and hummus factory. It has expanded and flourished with the revival of Northeast Minneapolis beginning in the late 1980s.

Continue south and cross 24th Avenue. In the Dovre Building is ❿ **Football Pizza** (formerly Crescent Moon Bakery), home of the "football pizza"—an Afghani flat, bubbly-crusted pie accompanied by a zippy chutney dipping sauce.

Before 22nd Avenue is ⓫ **La Colonia Restaurant,** featuring Ecuadorian and Colombian foods, including ceviche.

Continuing south, on the left are the New Boston Square Apartments—making one of the few references to the neighborhood's past.

Continue south under the railroad bridge and absorb the view of downtown Minneapolis.

After crossing 14th Avenue turn left.

Turn right on Tyler Street (there is no sidewalk) while walking carefully near the buildings. On the left is Crown Center, a complex of six rehabbed warehouse buildings that includes the superb German-inspired beers of ⓬ **Bauhaus Brew Labs.**

Turn left on Broadway Street.

Then turn right on Fillmore Street to finish the walk.

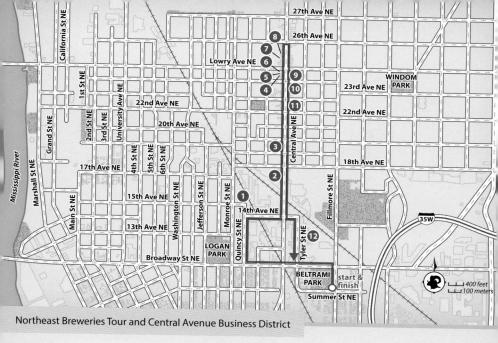

Northeast Breweries Tour and Central Avenue Business District

Points of Interest

1 **Indeed Brewing Company** indeedbrewing.com, 711 15th Ave. NE, Minneapolis, 612-843-5090

2 **Tattersall Distilling** tattersalldistilling.com, 1820 Central Ave. NE, #150, Minneapolis, 612-584-4152

3 **Maya Cuisine** facebook.com/mayacuisine, 1840 Central Ave. NE, Minneapolis, 612-789-0775

4 **El Taco Riendo** eltaco-riendo.com, 2420 Central Ave. NE, Minneapolis, 612-781-3000

5 **Costa Blanca Bistro** costablancabistro.com, 2416 Central Ave. NE, Minneapolis, 612-789-9296

6 **Sen Yai Sen Lek** senyai-senlek.com, 2422 Central Ave. NE, Minneapolis, 612-781-3046

7 **Fair State Brewing Cooperative** fairstate.coop, 2506-A Central Ave. NE, Minneapolis, 612-444-3200

8 **Aki's BreadHaus** akisbreadhaus.com, 2506 Central Ave. NE, Minneapolis, 612-578-7807

9 **Holy Land** holylandbrand.com, 2513 Central Ave. NE, Minneapolis, 612-781-2667

10 **Football Pizza** footballpizza.com, 2339 Central Ave. NE, Minneapolis, 612-782-0169

11 **La Colonia Restaurant** lacoloniarestaurant.com, 2205 Central Ave. NE. Minneapolis, 612-706-4146

12 **Bauhaus Brew Labs** bauhausbrewlabs.com, 1315 Tyler St. NE, Minneapolis, 612-276-6911

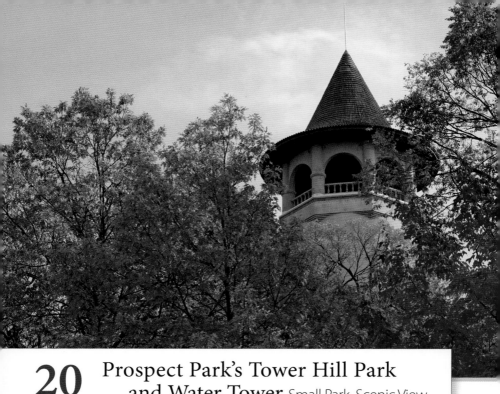

20 Prospect Park's Tower Hill Park and Water Tower Small Park, Scenic View

Above: The Witch's Hat water tower at Prospect Park

BOUNDARIES: Seymour Ave. SE, Orlin Ave. SE, Malcolm Ave. SE, University Ave. SE, Clarence Ave. SE
HUDSON'S TWIN CITIES STREET ATLAS COORDINATES: Map 394, 5C
DISTANCE: About 1.25 miles
DIFFICULTY: Strenuous
PARKING: Free parking on the south side of Seymour Ave. SE
PUBLIC TRANSIT: Bus lines 6 and 16; light rail

Prospect Park is an unusual neighborhood in Minneapolis, distinct in its piquant combination of hilly terrain, thick woods, and streets that weave throughout the upscale area. The hill that is today Tower Hill Park was created by a glacier 14,000 years ago. It was first settled in the 1880s, and the landmark Water Tower was erected in 1914. The housing stock has remained well preserved over the years, and the area is perennially home to academics from the nearby University of Minnesota.

The focal point of the neighborhood is ❶ **Tower Hill Park** and the view from atop its summit. The brief, but strenuous, walk provides arguably the best scenic overlook of downtown Minneapolis. Pack a picnic lunch, and then after the challenging walk, enjoy dining alfresco where the views of nature and the city are synchronized seamlessly.

Warning: Exercise extreme caution when descending the steep hill, and avoid it entirely when snow and ice are on the ground, making the path slick and impassable.

Walk Description

Begin by crossing Seymour Avenue Southeast between Clarence Avenue Southeast and Orlin Avenue Southeast and following the path that ascends the paved steps (closest to the tennis court) to the Water Tower. Take a left at the top of the stairs, just past the park bench.

Continue straight ahead up the next set of stairs. On the right is the Water Tower (1914) and a plaque commemorating Minneapolis city engineer Frederick Cappelen's alluring and functional design. To the left of the tower, park benches allow you to take in incredible views of the city. In the immediate foreground is the rooftop of Pratt Community School. A small part of the current structure was built in 1898. It is the oldest Minneapolis public school building still serving its original purpose. Beyond the neighborhood is the University of Minnesota, and in the background is the downtown Minneapolis skyline—you'll notice the IDS Center, the Wells Fargo Center, and Foshay Tower.

Upon reaching the first exit in the observation area, take a left and follow the steep path that descends the hill. *Warning:* Do not attempt to follow this path in icy months. Instead, when the weather is uncooperative, follow the second left for a gentler descent down the hill.

Continue following the edge of the woods downhill until you reach the sidewalk that parallels University Avenue Southeast.

Take a left on the sidewalk, and follow it to the corner of Malcolm Avenue Southeast.

Turn left to walk past the Prospect Park marker.

Turn right to cross University Avenue, following Malcolm Avenue Southeast. At the corner, be sure to observe the panoramic view of Prospect Park.

Follow Malcolm Avenue Southeast. Straight ahead is the ❷ **Surly Brewing Co.** and the attached Beer Hall and Restaurant. Opening in December 2014, Surly Nation first transformed the state's brewing laws by leading the effort to pass HR 1326, known as the Surly Bill, in 2011.

The Tower Hill Observation Deck: Open Once a Year

As if the panoramic view from Tower Hill wasn't exhilarating enough, the tower itself is open to the public during the annual Pratt Ice Cream Social. The event occurs the last week in May or the first week in June, thanks to the local neighborhood group Prospect Park East River Road Improvement Association. The ice-cream social embraces the area's diversity, serving not only ice cream but also bratwurst, egg rolls, and *sambusas* (a Somali version of samosas) on the Pratt Community School grounds.

The observation deck of Tower Hill provides the highlight of the evening. Open for only three hours a year, it offers a breathtaking view of Minneapolis from the 107-foot-high concrete structure that locals refer to as the "witch's hat" because of its immense conical roof. The tower is a local landmark, and the event is not to be missed.

In December 2014, their dream came true with a facility commensurate with their nationally recognized beer.

Turn around on Malcolm Avenue Southeast and return in the opposite direction.

On your right, as you carefully cross the U of M intercampus bus express line, about a block away was the Harris Machinery Warehouse. The once-dilapidated industrial site will be transformed into Malcolm Yards Market, a food hall. Preliminary plans for the site include an anchor restaurant and 17 smaller vendors. This venture and the burgeoning condo and apartment construction you're passing demonstrate the effect that the construction of the light rail and the Surly Brewing Co. has had on the neighborhood.

Continue straight, crossing University Avenue. Turn left and follow the sidewalk that parallels University Avenue. Across the street are the radio and television towers for KSTP. Turn right and follow Clarence Avenue Southeast as it borders the park. The path steeply ascends the hill.

Turn right on Seymour Avenue Southeast. Across the street are examples of the neighborhood's diverse yet fully integrated architecture. The Lowell Lamoreaux House (39 Seymour Ave. SE) is a lovely example of Shingle style, with an unusual granite porch. On this block modern and large Victorian homes fit together surprisingly well.

At the corner, turn right immediately onto the park path and follow it up the hill for another gorgeous view of the Water Tower. Turn left at the fork in front of the Water Tower. Turn left on the stairs and descend the path to return to Seymour Avenue Southeast, our starting point.

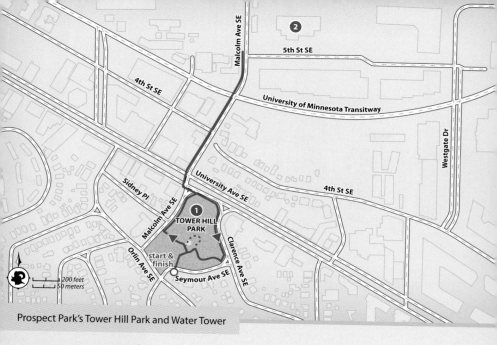

Prospect Park's Tower Hill Park and Water Tower

Points of Interest

1 **Tower Hill Park and Water Tower** pperr.org/history/thetower.html, 55 Malcolm Ave. SE, Minneapolis

2 **Surly Brewing Co.** surlybrewing.com, 520 Malcolm Ave. SE, Minneapolis, 763-999-4040

21 Minneapolis's Lake Street
Rich in Culture and History

Above: *View from the Martin Olav Sabo Bridge*

BOUNDARIES: Lake St. E., Chicago Ave. S., 26th St. E., Minnehaha Ave.
HUDSON'S TWIN CITIES STREET ATLAS COORDINATES: Map 394, 3D and 4D
DISTANCE: About 3 miles
DIFFICULTY: Moderate
PARKING: Free 3-hour parking at the 10th Ave. S. parking ramp with validation at the Midtown Global Market
PUBLIC TRANSIT: Numerous bus lines to Transit Center

This walk will take you through one of the most culturally vibrant and constantly changing sections of Minneapolis. The two crown jewels of the neighborhood are longtime resident Mercado Central and the much newer Midtown Global Market. Mercado Central was one of the first Latino marketplaces in the area, and many local Latino restaurateurs got their start renting a space in the mini-mall. Midtown Global Market is a cultural center representing more than two dozen countries and ethnic groups, with restaurants serving authentic dishes from Mexico, Vietnam, Morocco, Sweden, the Middle East, and Somalia, to name a few, as well as pan-fusion gourmet food that transcends borders. Vending kiosks offer clothes, jewelry, toys, knickknacks, and specialty deli and dessert items from just as many countries.

Walk Description

Start at the Transit Center just off the corner of Lake Street East and Chicago Avenue South. Across the street are ❶ **Uncle Hugo's Science Fiction Bookstore** (the oldest independent science fiction bookstore in the country) and Uncle Edgar's Mystery Bookstore.

Go straight past the Transit Center, heading away from Lake Street, and turn right at the first short set of stairs. Go down to the bottom of the big staircase and turn right onto the ❷ **Midtown Greenway.** To your left is ❸ **Freewheel Bike,** where you can buy or repair a bike or fix up your old one.

Go straight along the greenway approximately 1.25 miles until you get to 28th Street East. You'll see that navigating through Minneapolis via the greenway is easy, as street signs are located all along the path, and access to the upper street level can be found every quarter mile.

Cross 28th Street East at the crosswalk and take the left path.

Continue over the Martin Olav Sabo Bridge, named after the Minnesota Congressman. The design for this amazing cable-style bridge came from drawings first rendered by Croatian inventor Faust Vrancic in his book *Machinae Novae,* published in 1595. This is the first bridge in the country to be successfully built to Vrancic's design specifications. The Metro Blue Line runs directly underneath the bridge.

Take the first right to cross Hiawatha Avenue, and go straight west to follow 28th Street East. To your left is ❹ **Eco-Yard Midtown,** a prairie grassland restoration area and butterfly garden.

Turn left at 21st Ave. South and go south. This path takes you past the Green Institute, a nonprofit design group that creates eco-friendly building materials. Another prairie restoration project is along this path—this one filled with native grasses and wildflowers.

Cross 29th Street East and continue south.

Turn right at Lake Street East. This path parallels the ❺ **Minneapolis Pioneers and Soldiers Memorial Cemetery,** the oldest cemetery in Minneapolis. The land originally belonged to a man named Martin Layman (hence the original name, Layman's Cemetery), who began using the grounds for pauper burials in the 1850s. The cemetery was eventually closed in 1919 due to neglect, and it remained so until Minneapolis bought the grounds in 1928. Approximately

20,000 people are buried here, with only a quarter of the graves marked. A glimpse through the iron grates reveals ancient oak trees and weathered gravestones—some toppled over or broken beyond repair—marked by barely legible dates. The historic cemetery is open from April 15 to October 15.

Cross 16th Avenue South and keep going straight. Across the street and to your left is ❻ **Ingebretsen's Scandinavian Gifts,** which was founded in 1921 and remains the last operating vestige of that era. Formerly in disrepair, the neighborhood has seen new life, thanks to investments made by Latino business owners since the 1990s.

Midtown Global Market

The Midtown Greenway: Connecting the Mississippi River to Uptown

Opened in 2007, the Midtown Greenway is a combination bicycle and pedestrian path built on the remnants of the abandoned Milwaukee Road railway lines that once ran through the trench you're in now. The greenway is currently a little more than 5 miles long, but many more miles will be open to the public in the years ahead. Because of its location, pedestrians and cyclists can make their way through one of the busiest sections of south Minneapolis without having to stop for—or, for the most part, even see—a single car. Instead, travelers on the greenway are treated to community gardens, public art, and an underside view of dozens of historic bridges. The greenway is open 24 hours a day to commuters and is well lit at night, with emergency police call boxes located at regular intervals. During the winter, the path is regularly plowed to make it easily accessible for the die-hard pedestrians and bicyclists who brave the route even in the coldest months.

On the corner of 15th Avenue South and Lake Street East is ❼ **In the Heart of the Beast Puppet and Mask Theatre.** Every spring, the theater puts on a May Day parade that features bigger-than-life papier-mâché puppets portraying everything from butterflies and pagan goddesses to the latest figures in politics. The theater is also famous for contributing puppets to celebrations and political protest marches around the world.

Continue west down Lake Street and turn right on Elliot Avenue South. To your right is the ❽ **Midtown Global Market,** the jewel of this neighborhood. Located inside the former Sears building, dozens of kiosks sell deli items and merchandise from local farmers and international merchants, while some of the best restaurants in the Twin Cities have set up miniature offshoots here. Some of the can't-miss places include Tibet Arts & Gifts, with handmade textiles and jewelry at reasonable prices; Café Finspäng, which carries Scandinavian foods, books, and gifts; Panaderia El Mexicano, home of some of the prettiest cakes and tastiest flan in town; Manny's Tortas, which sells as-spicy-as-you-like-'em sandwiches; Salty Tart, which carries cakes and cookies way too good to share; La Loma, considered the home of the best tamales in town by just about every restaurant critic in the Twin Cities; and Los Ocampo, which makes Mexican food so authentic that many of the recipes are derived from 6,000-year-old Aztec delights.

Turn left by the parking lot to reach the Transit Center, the starting point.

Minneapolis's Lake Street

Points of Interest

① **Uncle Hugo's Science Fiction Bookstore/Uncle Edgar's Mystery Bookstore** unclehugo.com, 2864 Chicago Ave. S., Minneapolis, 612-824-6347/612-824-9984

② **Midtown Greenway** midtowngreenway.org, Abbott Ave. S. to W. River Pkwy. along Lake St. E., Minneapolis, 612-879-0103

③ **Freewheel Bike** freewheelbike.com, 2834 10th Ave. S., Minneapolis, 612-238-4447

④ **Eco-Yard Midtown** 2801 21st Ave. S., Minneapolis, 612-348-3777

⑤ **Minneapolis Pioneers and Soldiers Memorial Cemetery** friendsofthecemetery.org, 2945 Cedar Ave. S., Minneapolis, 612-729-8484

⑥ **Ingebretsen's Scandinavian Gifts** ingebretsens.com, 1601 Lake St. E., Minneapolis, 612-729-9333

⑦ **In the Heart of the Beast Puppet and Mask Theatre** hobt.org, 1500 Lake St. E., Minneapolis, 612-721-2535

⑧ **Midtown Global Market** midtownglobalmarket.org, 920 E. Lake St., Minneapolis, 612-872-4041

22 Minnehaha Parkway/48th and Chicago
Green Space, Relaxation Space

Above: *Lake Nokomis Park*

BOUNDARIES: Minnehaha Pkwy. E., Chicago Ave. S., 48th St. E., Nokomis Pkwy.
HUDSON'S TWIN CITIES STREET ATLAS COORDINATES: Map 421, 3B and 4B
DISTANCE: About 3 miles
DIFFICULTY: Moderate
PARKING: Free parking on Chicago Ave. S. and Minnehaha Pkwy. E.
PUBLIC TRANSIT: Bus lines 5, 14, 22, and 46

Three of the city's landmarks rich in natural geography combine for this walk: Minnehaha Parkway, a lovely section of the Grand Rounds Scenic Byway; a charming business district, 48th Street and Chicago in McRae Park; and Lake Nokomis. The proximity of nature and small town–like business districts is relatively common in the Twin Cities, but this walk stands out. Minnehaha Parkway is one of the seven byway districts in Minneapolis's Grand Rounds Scenic Byway.

Minnehaha Park passes through the neighborhood en route to Minnehaha Falls a few miles away, and just over the hill lies a quaint and quirky shopping district with numerous independently owned businesses. Nothing could be better on a hot summer day than enjoying organic ice cream at the Pumphouse Creamery after exploring the parkway and Lake Nokomis.

The scenic pathways on Minnehaha Parkway are slightly confusing, so pay close attention to the directions and map. Also, paths are categorized as bicycle-only, pedestrian-only, and combined. Parts of this walk are on the combined path—be aware of bicyclists zooming by, but most important, relax and enjoy the fresh air.

Walk Description

Begin at the southeast corner of Chicago Avenue South and Minnehaha Parkway East and walk south, crossing Minnehaha Creek.

Turn left immediately on the first path that wends through the woods, walking east. You can hear jets overhead on their way to and from nearby Minneapolis–St. Paul International Airport.

Turn left on the path that follows Minnehaha Creek, and take another left at 12th Avenue South to cross the stone bridge.

Cross 12th Avenue South, and then turn right on Minnehaha Parkway East. Follow the pedestrian path east along the creek, where a wetland restoration project is in place to prevent further erosion and improve water quality.

Continue east along the creek after the path intersects. Take in the wild irises and native plants ahead. The pedestrian and bike paths merge before Bloomington Avenue South, so be careful.

Go straight, continuing east, after crossing Bloomington Avenue South, and then go right as the path follows the creek. Continue on the winding path lined with pines, willows, and oaks.

Continue straight at the intersection with the bridge, and at the fork ahead, stay next to the creek. This part of the parkway is swampy lowland with reeds, red-winged blackbirds, and an abundance of flora and fauna.

After passing under the Cedar Avenue Bridge, continue along the creek.

Continue straight until you reach the parking lot and information kiosk at 2125 Minnehaha Ave.; then turn right to cross the pedestrian bridge.

Carefully cross Nokomis Parkway, and turn left to follow the pedestrian path as it curves along the lake. ❶ **Lake Nokomis Park** can be seen to the south through the trees. Continue south if you'd like to visit the seasonal ❷ **Sandcastle** restaurant (otherwise, follow the curve around the lake). Sandcastle offers scratch cooking on the beach and features beer, wine, food in a dog-friendly atmosphere, with gourmet sandwiches, hot dogs, and daily specials from chef Doug Flicker.

Cross the bridge; then after approximately 100 feet turn left on the pedestrian path and carefully cut across the bike path and Nokomis Parkway. In the opposite direction, about a quarter mile ahead on Nokomis Parkway, are the Nokomis Community Center and public restrooms.

After crossing Nokomis Parkway, follow the pedestrian path, and then turn left to cross the concrete bridge. On the left is the lock that the city can adjust to control the water level of Lake Nokomis—either stopping the water to fill the lake or allowing it to flow down the creek.

Turn left on the pedestrian path after passing the kiosk and parking lot again.

Turn right on the pedestrian path before going under the Cedar Avenue South Bridge. Follow the path to the corner of Cedar Avenue South and cross Minnehaha Parkway East.

Continue across Cedar and turn right across Minnehaha Parkway. Walk to the sidewalk of the service road and turn left, headed west through a lovely, tree-shaded residential area.

Continue west on Minnehaha Parkway East after crossing Bloomington Avenue South, where an eclectic architecture collection—from Tudors to modern eco-homes—lines the parkway.

Chicago Avenue street scene

Horace W. S. Cleveland: Father of the Grand Rounds National Scenic Byway

In the fledgling days of Minneapolis, landscape architect Horace W. S. Cleveland (1814–1900) had a keen sense of foresight, predicting the rise of a great city and recognizing the importance of purchasing parklands for public use. His later civil engineering accomplishments include the parkway system in Omaha, Nebraska, and Sleepy Hollow Cemetery in Concord, Massachusetts.

The Grand Rounds, a linked series of park areas, are some of Minneapolis's greatest civic assets. The byway runs through seven districts: the Mississippi River, Theodore Wirth, Northeast, Chain of Lakes, Victory Memorial, Downtown Riverfront, and Minnehaha. With 50.1 miles, and more land being acquired for walking, biking, and driving, this system is recognized as one of the nation's best. The Minnehaha byway is 12.8 miles of multiuse green space and parkway along the creek. Cleveland's legacy is felt daily by Minneapolitans enjoying the city's extensive scenic byways.

Turn right on Chicago Avenue South, and walk up the steep hill toward the McRae Park business district. Continue on Chicago Avenue South, descending the hill. After crossing 48th Street East turn left, and turn left again to walk in the opposite direction on Chicago Avenue South. North of 48th Street East on Chicago Avenue South is arguably the Twin Cities' best ice-cream parlor, ❸ **Pumphouse Creamery**, where a rotating selection of 20 organic ice creams and sorbets delights the taste buds—whether strawberry, banana, or mouthwatering local cherry. A few doors down is one of three locations of the local leader in baking, ❹ **Turtle Bread Company.** Since 1994, it has offered up fresh breads, cakes, pies, cookies, and pastries, as well as sandwiches, homemade soups, and breakfast.

After crossing 48th Street East you'll come to another block of fine foods and entertainment. First is ❺ **Town Hall Tap,** with excellent beer crafted in-house and equally excellent food. On the right is Parkway Theater, a collaboration between two local mainstays: the 1931 ❻ **Parkway Theater** and ❼ **Pepito's** Mexican restaurant. Since its inception in 1971, the restaurant has served Mexican-American favorites such as tacos, enchiladas, burritos, and even chicken mole in a friendly and cozy environment. Pepito's also owns the theater, which serves beer, wine, and food.

Continue to ascend and then descend Chicago Avenue South to finish the walk.

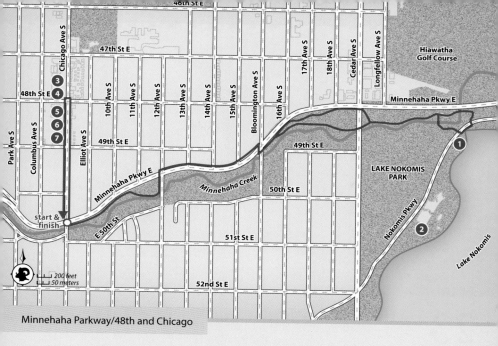

Minnehaha Parkway/48th and Chicago

Points of Interest

1 **Lake Nokomis Park** minneapolisparks.org, 4955 W. Lake Nokomis Pkwy., Minneapolis, 612-370-4923

2 **Sandcastle** sandcastlempls.com, 4955 W. Lake Nokomis Pkwy., Minneapolis, 612-722-5550

3 **Pumphouse Creamery** pumphouse-creamery.com, 4754 Chicago Ave. S., Minneapolis, 612-825-2021

4 **Turtle Bread Company** turtlebread.com, 4782 Chicago Ave. S., Minneapolis, 612-823-7333

5 **Town Hall Tap** townhalltap.com, 4810 Chicago Ave. S., Minneapolis, 612-767-7307

6 **Parkway Theater** theparkwaytheater.com, 4814 Chicago Ave. S., Minneapolis, 612-822-3030

7 **Pepito's** pepitosrestaurant.com, 4820 Chicago Ave. S., Minneapolis, 612-822-2104

23 Minnehaha Falls
"Of the Lovely Laughing Waters"

Above: *Minnehaha Falls*

BOUNDARIES: 50th St. E., Hiawatha Ave., Godfrey Pkwy., Mississippi River
HUDSON'S TWIN CITIES STREET ATLAS COORDINATES: Map 421, 5B; Map 422, 1B
DISTANCE: About 2.25 miles
DIFFICULTY: Moderate
PARKING: Free parking on Minnehaha Ave. S.
PUBLIC TRANSIT: Bus line 7; light rail at the 50th St. Minnehaha Park Station

If you're a fan of Henry Wadsworth Longfellow's poetry, or simply interested in 19th-century Americana in general, then a stop at ❶ **Minnehaha Regional Park** is an absolute must. The falls, which share the name of Longfellow's tragically fated heroine (it's Dakota for "laughing waters"), were a major tourist attraction long before the area was designated as parkland in 1883. In the spring and summer, visitors are treated to picturesque waterfalls cascading over a tree-lined chasm and into Minnehaha Creek below; in the wintertime, the falls are frozen into glistening blue, white, and green gigantic icicles. They're probably not the tallest waterfalls you'll ever see, but they are unique in their surroundings—an exquisite park with waterfalls, wildflowers, sandstone cliffs, and big, open wilderness spaces, all located in the heart of a busy metropolis.

Note: During the winter, all the staircases leading to the bottom of the falls are closed. It's still worth a visit to see the frozen waterfalls from the top, even if you can't get down to the lower paths.

Walk Description

Start in front of the ❷ **John H. Stevens House.** It's the little white house in the park, located right off of Minnehaha Park Drive and 50th Street East. Built in 1850, it was Minneapolis's very first house. It was originally where the downtown Minneapolis Post Office building is now but was moved here in 1890; after eventually being refurbished, it reopened to the public in the 1980s.

Facing the Stevens House, turn left to head into the park. This route takes you under the canopy of the vine-covered pergola. Native plants and flowers, including trilliums, wood poppies, and columbines, surround both sides of the structure. The right side looks out over the bluffs leading down to Minnehaha Creek.

Go straight past the first set of stairs and go down the second set to your right. You are now walking directly over the top of Minnehaha Falls. If you look to the left while crossing the bridge, you'll get a glimpse of the bronze statue commemorating the love of Hiawatha and Minnehaha.

Turn right at the bottom of the stairs. Follow the retaining wall until you get to the next set of stairs, located on your right. Before heading down the stairs, stop and take a look at the falls. From way up here, you get a spectacular view of them cascading into Minnehaha Creek below, as well as the grotto hollowed out by the pounding force of the water. Behind you is the picnic pavilion, which has indoor tables, restrooms, water fountains, soda machines, and bicycle rentals. The pavilion is also home to ❸ **Sea Salt Eatery,** one of the best seafood restaurants in the Twin Cities.

Go all the way down to the bottom of the winding staircase, and turn right. This spot offers the best view of the scope of Minnehaha Falls. The stairs and masonry along this path were initiated by the Works Progress Administration in the 1930s.

Turn left to cross the little stone bridge, and left again onto the dirt path that follows the Minnehaha Creek, to your left; notice the amazing limestone and sandstone cliffs on the right.

At the next bridge, take the far-right path into the woods. This area is home to some of Minnesota's most beautiful wildflowers, including orchidlike, orange-spotted touch-me-nots and tiny, blue-and-yellow forget-me-nots.

Turn left at the bridge. To the right of the bridge you'll see a boardwalk path leading into the woods. If you're feeling adventurous, take the path to the banks of the Mississippi River. However, it's very rustic and often flooded in the spring and anytime after a heavy rainstorm.

Cross the bridge and take a left at the fork. At the next fork, go left to follow the creek. Turn left to go down the hill. Here's where the path ends. If the weather is warm and you feel like taking a dip, the water is rarely more than knee-deep, making it a popular wading spot.

Turn right to go through the grassy field. At the far end of the field, you'll see an asphalt path that you'll want to take uphill. At the top of the hill, turn right. At the next fork, turn left. At the corner next to the VETERANS HOME sign at 46th Avenue South, turn right to cross the street.

Go straight to follow Godfrey Parkway on the combined bicycle/pedestrian path. On your left and right are prairie restoration areas, where prairie grass and wildflowers such as daylilies, coneflowers, and daisies have been planted.

Go under the bridge and keep going straight. Take the first right and cross the parking lot to the UPPER MISSISSIPPI RIVER LOCK AND DAM NO. 1 sign. Turn right to go down the hill and under the Ford Bridge. This path takes you close to the Mississippi River and its neighboring bluffs.

Go down to ❹ **Lock & Dam No. 1** (commonly known as Ford Dam)**.** From here, you can see the twin lock and dam to your right, while across the river are the buff-colored buildings of the Ford Hydroelectric Plant. You can fish off the steps here if you have a fishing license.

Plantings at Longfellow Gardens

Turn around and follow the path to the right, back to the top of the hill. Go straight until you reach the Park & Recreation Board kiosk. This sign has information about the history and purpose of the lock and dam.

Turn left and go straight to cross the lock-and-dam entrance road. Keep straight under the bridge. At the end of the block, take the left fork. Go straight to continue following Godfrey Parkway. Keep following the path around, past the playground and to the front parking lot. When the path splits, turn left.

Follow the path and cross Minnehaha Avenue. Turn right. To your left is the yellow ❺ **Longfellow House,** a two-thirds-scale replica of Henry Wadsworth Longfellow's house in Cambridge, Massachusetts. Robert "Fish" Jones, famous fishmonger, showman, and entrepreneur, was a huge Longfellow fan and had the house built in 1906. Over the years, the house has served as a zoo, a library, a haunted house, and, in its current role, an office for the Park Board.

Sculpture of Minnehaha and Hiawatha by Jacob Fjelde

Follow the path around the house and up the hill. Turn left into ❻ **Longfellow Gardens.** Take the next immediate left and follow the path through the garden. Longfellow Gardens was also run by Fish Jones, who used the grounds as a zoo, an amusement park, and formal gardens.

After the gardens, head toward the staircase by the Longfellow House. Go down the stairs and straight to cross the train tracks. Go straight and cross Minnehaha Avenue South, and then turn right to follow Minnehaha Park Drive South. Across the street is the ❼ **Minnehaha Depot,** a little brown train depot that is also called the Princess Depot because of its dainty size and design. Built in 1875, the depot was one of three stops on Minnesota's first railroad and, in its heyday, handled nearly 40 trains a day. Today, it serves as a mini museum for the park and the railway system.

Directly ahead is the white Stevens House, the starting point.

Points of Interest

1 **Minnehaha Regional Park** minneapolissparks.org, 4801 Minnehaha Park Dr. S., Minneapolis, 612-230-6400

2 **John H. Stevens House** johnhstevenshouse.org, 4901 Minnehaha Ave. S., Minneapolis, 612-722-2220

3 **Sea Salt Eatery** seasalteatery.com, 4825 Minnehaha Ave. S., Minneapolis, 612-721-8990

4 **Lock & Dam No. 1 (Ford Dam)** tinyurl.com/lockdam1, 5000 Godfrey Pkwy., Minneapolis

5 **Longfellow House** minneapolissparks.org, 4800 Minnehaha Ave. S., Minneapolis, 612-230-6520

6 **Longfellow Gardens** minneapolissparks.org, 3933 Minnehaha Pkwy. E., Minneapolis, 612-230-6400

7 **Minnehaha Depot** transportationmuseum.org, 4801 Minnehaha Ave. S., Minneapolis, 651-228-0263

24 Highland Park and Hidden Falls Regional Park Nature, Shopping, and Dining

Above: *View of the Ford Dam*

BOUNDARIES: Mississippi River, Pinehurst Ave. W., Kenneth St., Elsie Ln.
HUDSON'S TWIN CITIES STREET ATLAS COORDINATES: Map 422, 1B, 2B, and 1C
DISTANCE: About 4.5 miles
DIFFICULTY: Moderate
PARKING: Free parking on Cleveland Ave.
PUBLIC TRANSIT: Bus lines 54, 83, 87, and 134

Highland Park is one of St. Paul's most affluent neighborhoods. It has an abundance of natural and cultural amenities, thanks to its location atop an idyllic bluff east of the Mississippi River and its diverse population. The Ford Twin Cities Assembly Plant called the area home from 1925 until it closed in 2012. Minnesota baseball legends who played or lived in the area as kids include Jack Morris, Dave Winfield, Paul Molitor, and Joe Mauer, 2006 American League Batting Champion of the Minnesota Twins. Highland Park is also a historic neighborhood for St. Paul's Jewish population, including Orthodox and Lubavitch Hasidim groups.

Beneath the surface, however, this upscale community has been the scene of an unusually large number of famous crimes: It was a Prohibition-era drinking stop and gangster hangout as well as the site of St. Paul's most infamous murder, the 1963 T. Eugene Thompson case. A more recent high-profile example is that of Sara Jane Olson, also known as Kathleen Soliah in the Symbionese Liberation Army, who pled guilty in 2001 to possessing explosives with intent to murder, after living as a fugitive here for 23 years. This odd David Lynch–like juxtaposition of good and evil in Highland Park adds another dimension to an otherwise placid community.

Walk Description

Begin at the southeast corner of Bohland Avenue and Cleveland Avenue South, and walk north on Cleveland Avenue.

Turn right on Ford Parkway. The ❶ **Highland Village Center** features local and national chain stores, plus a few neighborhood businesses. ❷ **Highland Café & Bakery** specializes in breakfast foods, such as waffles and omelets, as well as soups and sandwiches for lunch and dinner.

Turn left on Kenneth Street; then turn left on Ford Parkway and return on the opposite side of Kenneth Street. On the right, the Highland business district resumes at ❸ **Half Price Books,** a national used-book store with a wide selection of books, records, CDs, and DVDs.

Turn right on Cleveland Avenue South, where the classic marquee of the ❹ **Highland 1 & 2** theater dominates the small-town feel of the street. On the right is ❺ **TeaSource,** premium purveyors of imported teas. Right next door is ❻ **Menchie's,** a national chain that offers serve-your-own frozen yogurt with an assortment of toppings.

Turn left at Pinehurst Avenue West, and turn left again on Cleveland Avenue South to return to Ford Parkway. This block includes excellent choices for anything from a small nosh and coffee to an all-you-can-eat buffet. ❼ **Cleveland Wok** falls into the latter category, with an extensive and inexpensive high-quality Chinese and Vietnamese buffet. ❽ **Highland Grill** serves American comfort food for breakfast, lunch, and dinner.

Turn right on Ford Parkway. The grade descends steeply after crossing Cretin Avenue South. The area on the left is the site of the recently demolished Ford Motor Company production plant. Constructed in 1925 to produce Model Ts, it was later remodeled to accommodate technology changes in the auto-assembly industry. Placed on the market in December 2017, the 122-acre parcel of land overlooking the Mississippi River now presents a redevelopment opportunity for the city of St. Paul and the Highland Park neighborhood.

Nearing the Mississippi River on Ford Parkway, turn right on the path descending the hill next to the Intercity (Ford) Bridge—one of four concrete arch bridges linking Minneapolis and St. Paul.

After carefully crossing Mississippi River Boulevard, turn left. The path provides a breathtaking view of the river. Behind the sumac and in the river is ❾ **Lock & Dam No. 1,** commonly known as Ford Dam. Constructed in 1917, the concrete dam is 574 feet long and 30 feet high. The dam played an important role in the effort to improve the once nearly impassable Mississippi River between downtown St. Paul and Minneapolis. Next to the dam is the hydroelectric plant, which Ford recently sold to Brookfield Power, a Canadian energy firm. Originally built to supply power for the assembly plant, the hydroelectric plant was a significant factor in luring Ford to the neighborhood in the 1920s.

Follow the path on the right to the Ford Dam Scenic Overlook, where you have a phenomenal vista of the Mississippi River. Across the river are several of the 22 Minnesota Historic Veterans Home buildings. The first eight were constructed as early as 1888 in the Richardsonian

The Highland 1 & 2 theater shows first-run feature films.

Romanesque style. The 51-acre VA Home sits nestled on the Mississippi, surrounded by Minnehaha Regional Park. Continue approximately 0.5 mile, following the pedestrian path on the bluff above the river through a vast network of forests and floodplains.

Turn right on the pedestrian path on Mississippi River Boulevard, curving around the falls, which become increasingly louder as you approach them. Before reaching the falls on the right is an excellent—though barely visible from the path—scenic overlook down a flight of stone steps. Continue on the path, passing Hidden Falls and approaching Hidden Falls Regional Park.

Turn right after crossing Hidden Falls Drive, and descend the steep pedestrian path on the street. Continue following the path downhill. The picnic pavilion and public restrooms are to the right across the street. Continue following the path south as it snakes below the bluff, and turn left as the path forks. On the right is the Mississippi River and public boat access.

Turn around and return in the opposite direction after taking in the river view. **10 Hidden Falls Regional Park,** which comprises more than 130 acres and 6.7 miles of trails, merits its own nature walk.

Continue to follow the path north along the river bluff; when the path forks, turn right to ascend the steep grade. At the top of the hill, turn right on Mississippi River Boulevard. Look down the hill at Hidden Falls Regional Park. The view along this path is truly breathtaking; take a moment to look across the river at Fort Snelling and watch the planes at Minneapolis–St. Paul International Airport.

Turn left on Elsie Lane as it crosses the working-class residential area Highland Park. In the late 1830s, four homes in this then-secluded area across the river from Fort Snelling formed Old Rum Town, where soldiers, trappers, and other transients imbibed clandestine cocktails. However, the homes on this block were built in the mid-20th century and lack a sidewalk, so walk carefully on this quiet neighborhood street.

Turn left on Cleveland Avenue South. This section of Highland Park contains well-maintained, modest homes. Continue north, crossing the railroad bridge. On the left is the Ford Little League Park, where Minnesota Twins catcher/first baseman Joe Mauer; three-time 20-game winner Jack Morris; former Minnesota Vikings Pro-Bowl center Matt Birk; and countless other kids played baseball. The park closed because of high arsenic levels in 2007 but reopened in spring 2008.

Head north on Cleveland Avenue South to finish the walk. On the right are the Highland Village Apartments, 12 lovely Colonial Revival–style apartments.

Highland Park and Hidden Falls Regional Park

Points of Interest

1. **Highland Village Center** bloomcommercial.com/highland, 2024 Ford Pkwy., St. Paul
2. **Highland Café & Bakery** highlandcafeandbakery.com, 2012 Ford Pkwy., St. Paul, 651-698-3400
3. **Half Price Books** hpb.com, 2041 Ford Pkwy., St. Paul, 651-699-1391
4. **Highland 1 & 2** manntheatresmn.com, 760 Cleveland Ave. S., St. Paul, 651-698-3085
5. **TeaSource** teasource.com, 752 Cleveland Ave. S., St. Paul, 651-690-9822
6. **Menchie's** menchies.com, 750 Cleveland Ave. S., St. Paul, 651-797-6428
7. **Cleveland Wok** clevelandwok.com, 767 Cleveland Ave. S., St. Paul, 651-699-3141
8. **Highland Grill** highlandgrill.com, 771 Cleveland Ave. S., St. Paul, 651-690-1173
9. **Lock & Dam No. 1 (Ford Dam)** tinyurl.com/lockdam1, 5000 Godfrey Pkwy., Minneapolis
10. **Hidden Falls Regional Park** tinyurl.com/hiddenfallsregionalpark, 1313 Hidden Falls Dr., St. Paul, 651-632-5111

25 West Seventh Street

Above: *The Schmidt Brewing complex*

BOUNDARIES: Randolph Ave., W. Seventh St., Jefferson Ave.
HUDSON'S TWIN CITY STREET ATLAS COORDINATES: Map 422, 5A, 5B, 4A, and 4B
DISTANCE: About 1 mile
DIFFICULTY: Easy
PARKING: Free parking on Jefferson Ave. and Duke St.
PUBLIC TRANSIT: Bus lines 54 and 74

Below the bluffs on the flats, West Seventh Street, also known as Fort Road, cuts through the street grid, running roughly parallel with the Mississippi. Fort Road's original route predated St. Paul by decades and more closely followed the series of hills that dominates the riverine section between downtown St. Paul and Fort Snelling until it was relocated to the present route in the 1850s.

West Seventh's history was working-class, with beer brewing a major business, thanks to the Mount Simon-Hinckley aquifer's 35,000-year-old water. The wells lead directly to Fountain Cave

(In-Yan Ti-Pi, in the Dakota language), where Pierre "Pig's Eye" Parrant, founder of St. Paul, sold whiskey to pioneers and soldiers. The first brewery in the area, in the 1850s, was Stahlmann Cave Brewery. Later, Jacob Schmidt Brewing quenched the thirst of growing numbers. The sprawling complex by famed Chicago brewery architect Bernard Barthel was constructed in 1901.

Schmidt Brewing was locally owned until 1955. First, Detroit's Pfeiffer Brewing Company purchased the brewery, and then G. Heileman Brewing Company purchased it in 1972. The brewery reorganized on a smaller scale as the Minnesota Brewing Company from 1991 to 2002, with Landmark and Pig's Eye Pilsner as its flagship beers. But eventually it, too, closed.

In recent years, the area has reemerged as a quirky neighborhood, melding an indoor aquaponic fish and produce farm with tattoo parlors, bars and restaurants, and art studios. The neighborhood's progress is exemplified by the forthcoming Keg and Case marketplace, scheduled to open in 2018. The 30,000-square-foot food hall will have a year-round farmers market, a brewery, a taproom, and house-made ice cream. In the meantime, the best years of West Seventh, and a renaissance, are on the horizon.

Walk Description

Start at the southwest corner of Jefferson Avenue and West Seventh Street, and head southwest on West Seventh. Across the street is the massive former Schmidt Brewing Company, which you will pass on the way back. After Oneida Street on the right is the historic ❶ **Marie Schmidt-Bremer Home.** Marie, the daughter of Jacob Schmidt, married banker Adolf Bremer. The couple's 34-year-old son, Edward, was kidnapped by the infamous Karpis-Barker gang in 1934; he survived only after a large ransom was paid. However, the victory proved Pyrrhic for the gang. Doggedly pursued by the FBI, within months the leading members were captured or killed. Today, the building serves as a halfway house and is said to be haunted by a brunette woman in a white dress.

The preexisting angle of Fort Road defined the superimposed grid; hence the oddly shaped blocks, with only three lots on this block and two businesses on the next. Continue on Seventh—always West Seventh (the West End). The neighborhood boasts an eclectic mix of coffee shops, tattoo parlors, pawn shops, and art galleries—such as one owned by former St. Paul city councilman Dave Thune—as well as a barbershop that's more than a century old, bars, restaurants, and funky antiques stores.

At the corner of James Avenue and Daly Street is ❷ **Center for Lost Objects,** an exemplar of the emerging neighborhood, showcasing a rotating collection of unusual art.

After James Avenue is ❸ **Supatra's Thai Cuisine**—authentic fare with a pleasant outside patio. ❹ **Shamrocks: The Irish Nook,** is a St. Paul classic featuring specialty burgers such as the

West 7th and ones named after local sports legends such as Matt Birk, Paul Molitor, Joe Mauer. It's owned by Casper's and Runyon's Nook, 1.5 miles west on Randolph Avenue, across from Cretin-Derham Hall High School.

Turn left at Randolph Avenue and immediately left again on 7th Street. On the right, past Toronto Street, is the massive former Schmidt Brewing complex—soon to be the **⑤ Keg and Case** marketplace. Spanning from Webster Street to Oneida Street, the rehabbed complex also houses the **⑥ Schmidt Artist Lofts,** which comprise the six-floor Brewhouse building and the four-floor Bottlehouse building.

If you're thirsty and have your own container, you can fill up at **⑦ The Drink,** which dispenses water from the aquifer for $1 per gallon. The provider, innovative aquaponics company Urban Organics, started out by engineering an eco-friendly system for farming fish and produce in the Hamm's building and expanded to the old Schmidt site in June 2017. With 87,000 square feet, the second site is 10 times larger than the first and will supply organic arctic char and Atlantic salmon, as well as arugula, kale, and bok choy, to the Twin Cities.

Continue to Jefferson Avenue to complete the walk.

Window display at The Center for Lost Objects art gallery

Points of Interest

1. **Marie Schmidt-Bremer Home** 855 W. 7th St., St. Paul

2. **Center for Lost Objects Gallery & Showroom** centerforlostobjects.com, 957 W. 7th St., St. Paul, 651-504-2356

3. **Supatra's Thai Cuisine** supatra.com, 967 W. 7th St., St. Paul, 651-222-5859

4. **Shamrocks: The Irish Nook** crnook.com, 995 W. 7th St., St. Paul, 651-228-9925

5. **Keg and Case** kegandcase.com or facebook.com/kegandcase, 928 W. 7th St., St. Paul

6. **Schmidt Artist Lofts** schmidtartistlofts.com, 900 W. 7th St., St. Paul, 651-842-2980

7. **The Drink** the-drink.com, 888 W 7th St., St. Paul, 651-451-5921

26 High Bridge and Cherokee Regional Park

Above: View of the St. Paul riverfront from the High Bridge

BOUNDARIES: Curtice St. W., Smith Ave., W. Seventh St., Cherokee Heights Blvd.
HUDSON'S TWIN CITIES STREET ATLAS COORDINATES: Map 422, 5A and 5B
DISTANCE: 3 miles
DIFFICULTY: Strenuous
PARKING: Free parking along Cliff St.
PUBLIC TRANSIT: Bus line 62

The High Bridge connects West Seventh Street and Cherokee Regional Park. The bridge reflects its name: it is the highest bridge on the Mississippi River in Minneapolis and St. Paul. With a 4% grade, it is 0.5 mile long with a 160-foot deck height. The current bridge was constructed in 1987. The first bridge (1889) was replaced after a tornado/severe storm struck, and was rebuilt in 1904. Today, the new bridge affords a breathtaking vantage point of the Mississippi River, St. Paul, and the surrounding area.

Cherokee Regional Park began as a tourist campground hatched by James J. Hill and became a public park by the mid-1920s. In recent years, the West Seventh vicinity has developed a brewing district in keeping with the region's heritage. First, Bad Weather Brewing Company relocated here from the Lucid Brewing facility in Minnetonka in 2015. Then, the Anthony Waldmann pre–Civil War lager house was renovated. The Waldmann Brewery & Wurstery revisits the time when German lager technology based on cool fermentation and cold storage transformed expectations of what was considered good beer. Today, craft brewers' talent is measured on the India Pale Ale (IPA) and countless creative and revived styles—the cold clear style of the malt-forward lager was all the rage in 1857, when the saloon originally opened. After completing this challenging walk, imbibe in a lager that transports you to that time.

Walk Description

Start at Cliff Street and Smith Avenue, and ascend the steep grade of the High Bridge. Breathe in an unparalleled panoramic view of downtown St. Paul to the northwest and Shepard Road, the bluffs, and the former Schmidt Brewing Company in the distance to the southeast. Then look down from the height of the bridge at the Mississippi River traffic below.

Turn right on Cherokee Avenue and follow the sidewalk; take a seat on one of the numerous benches, or stroll above the river.

Go right, and stay on the path (tennis courts are on the left) as the blacktop path continues, following the bluff.

Continue on the path as it runs parallel to Cherokee Heights Boulevard. ❶ **Cherokee Regional Park** is now on both sides of the path.

Before the handicap-parking area, follow the pedestrian sidewalk cutout and turn left. Proceed due east between the picnic area and basketball court, or explore the 100-acre park. More than 300,000 visitors annually enjoy its picnic and recreation amenities. Pass between the bathrooms and playground heading up the hill. Then, at the CHEROKEE PARK sign, turn left and follow the sidewalk.

Turn left on Chippewa Avenue and continue north until Chippewa meets Baker Street. Turn right to follow the Baker Street sidewalk. Follow Baker Street east and turn left on Cherokee Avenue. Observe the scenic vista—especially after the foliage has fallen from the trees—when the splendor of the Cathedral of Saint Paul and the Minnesota State Capitol is in view. Cross Ottawa Avenue and then take an immediate right on the sidewalk that follows George Street.

Food trucks often park outside Bad Weather Brewing Company's taproom.

At the stoplight, cross Smith Avenue and take an immediate left. Enjoy the view descending the hill.

Continue on Smith and cross Cherokee Avenue. Before beginning the walk across the bridge, check out the observation deck on the right. On the bridge is a breathtaking view of downtown St. Paul, Harriet Island, and the St. Paul Yacht Club. At the end of the bridge on the sidewalk, pass the sculpture garden.

Turn left on Seventh Street and turn left on Smith Avenue. If you're thirsty for an excellent craft beer, then proceed to ❷ **Bad Weather Brewing Company** straight ahead on McBoal Street. Returning to Smith Avenue, turn right. Just ahead on the right is ❸ **Waldmann Brewery & Wurstery.** The saloon is furnished for time travel to the antebellum era, with oil lamps, thick and distorted glass windowpanes, and acoustic music. Return to Cliff Street to complete the walk.

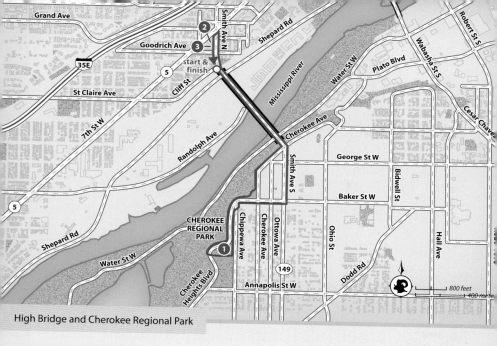

High Bridge and Cherokee Regional Park

Points of Interest

① **Cherokee Regional Park** 700 Cherokee Heights Blvd., St. Paul, 651-632-5111

② **Bad Weather Brewing Company** badweatherbrewery.com, 414 7th St. W., St. Paul, 651-207-6627

③ **Waldmann Brewery & Wurstery** waldmannbrewery.com, 445 Smith Ave., St. Paul, 651-222-1857

27 Cathedral, Ramsey, and Summit Hills
Linking August Past with Dynamic Present

Above: The James J. Hill House

BOUNDARIES: Summit Ave., Lexington Pkwy. N., Dayton Ave.
HUDSON'S TWIN CITIES STREET ATLAS COORDINATES: Map 395, 5D; Map 422, 4A and 5A
DISTANCE: About 4.25 miles
DIFFICULTY: Moderate
PARKING: Free parking on Summit Ave.
PUBLIC TRANSIT: Bus lines 21, 63, and 74

The Cathedral, Ramsey, and Summit Hills area—often referred to simply as the Hill District—was recognized by the National Register of Historic Places in 1976 and is acknowledged for some of the best-preserved Victorian homes in the country. However, it fell into hard times in the Depression years of the 1930s and did not recover until the late '60s, when urban pioneers purchased the homes, often for a fraction of their value, and restored them to their architectural glory. Located on the bluff above downtown St. Paul, the first mansions were built on Summit

Hill in the 1850s, but many of the eclectic Victorian mansions were built in the 1880s. James J. Hill, the railroad-tycoon creator of the Great Northern Railway, built his massive red sandstone mansion in 1891.

Another landmark, the Cathedral of Saint Paul, an architectural tribute to St. Peter's Basilica in Rome, was completed in 1915. Standing 306.5 feet above downtown, it looms over Cathedral Hill like an immense colossus of St. Cloud (Minnesota) granite. In its shadow lies a substantial business district, as well as apartment and condo buildings on Selby Avenue, a development legacy from when the long-gone streetcar system first connected the neighborhood to downtown in 1887. In the past 20 years, the Selby Avenue business district has become a hotbed for dining, drinking, and shopping. In 1976, W. A. Frost & Company helped jump-start the area's renaissance, which continues even today.

Walk Description

Begin at the southeast corner of Summit Avenue and Nina Street, and walk southwest down Summit Avenue to overlook downtown. This section of the street contains one notable home after another: even when the architecture is typical of a style, other distinctions are striking. On the left, the 1858 Stewart-Driscoll House (312 Summit Ave.), an Italian–style mansion, is the oldest house on Summit Avenue. The next few homes, again on the left, are early Cass Gilbert works. Gilbert later designed the Minnesota State Capitol, the US Supreme Court, and the Woolworth Building in New York City. The William Lightner House (1893), at 318 Summit Ave., is an interesting combination of Richardsonian Romanesque and Classical Revival, while the William Lightner–George Young Double House (1888), at 322–24 Summit Ave., draws from Queen Anne and Renaissance Revival.

Continue west on Summit Avenue, passing a fine collection of eclectic Victorian homes. Straight ahead on the left, where Ramsey Street merges at the top of the hill and becomes Summit Avenue, is ❶ Summit Overlook Park—stop for a panoramic view of St. Paul.

After crossing Ramsey Street, turn right on Summit Avenue. Around the corner are a number of exceptional mansions. The University Club (420 Summit Ave.) is an excellent example of Tudor Revival architecture, built in 1913. Another impressive mansion is the limestone, Italianate-style Burbank-Livingston-Griggs House (432 Summit Ave.) from 1863.

Continue on Summit Avenue and notice the interesting combination of architectural styles. The Summit Terrace (587–601 Summit Ave.) brownstone row house was the residence of F. Scott Fitzgerald when he wrote his first novel, *This Side of Paradise.*

James J. Hill: Railroad Tycoon of the Gilded Age

James J. Hill was an influential St. Paul businessman whose impact is still felt today. Hill was born of modest means in Ontario, Canada, in 1838. He started out in St. Paul working as a transportation clerk for riverboats on the levee of the Mississippi River. In 1878 Hill set out to make his fortune in the fledgling railroad industry, purchasing the nearly bankrupt St. Paul and Pacific Railroad with other financial partners. He quickly turned the railroad's finances around and added routes to Canada, the Rocky Mountains, and the West Coast. His business interests diversified into agriculture, shipping, mining, milling, finance, and banking. The companies he developed still exist today, after mergers and consolidations, as Burlington Northern Santa Fe Railroad and U.S. Bank. His legacy also continues in philanthropy—particularly the James J. Hill Reference Library in downtown St. Paul, a nonprofit, independent library founded in 1921.

Continue west. After several blocks of lovely Victorians, you come to the Tudor Revival–style ❷ **Minnesota Governor's Residence** (1006 Summit Ave.), which has served the state's chief executive since the late 1960s.

Turn right on Lexington Parkway, then immediately turn right to return on the opposite side of Summit Avenue. The corner is dominated by the immense and spectacular Italian and French Romanesque–inspired ❸ **Saint Thomas More Catholic Community** (1925).

Continue along Summit Avenue to cross Milton Street, the location of ❹ **Mitchell Hamline School of Law,** formerly the William Mitchell College of Law. The Warren East. Burger Library is named for the school's best-known alumnus, who was appointed by Richard Nixon in 1969 and served until 1986 as chief justice of the US Supreme Court.

Continue east into another impressive section of Summit Avenue's mansion row. In 1908, St. Paul architect Clarence Johnston designed the colossal Samuel and Madeline Dittenhofer House (807 Summit Ave.), as well as 37 other homes on Summit Avenue. He also created the William Elsinger House (701 Summit Ave.); it is immediately preceded by the Jacob and Bettie Dittenhofer House (705 Summit Ave.), designed by Cass Gilbert.

Cross Dale Street and turn left. Observe the variation in housing stock as you walk away from Summit Avenue.

Turn right on Selby Avenue. Kitty-corner is the ❺ **Mississippi Market,** a fantastic local co-op without a membership requirement. After crossing Kent Street is ❻ **Revival,** purveyor of fried chicken and other Southern treats—this is the larger of two locations, the first being its crazy-busy location in south Minneapolis. Across the street is ❼ **Ten Thousand Villages,** a store selling arts and crafts made by artisans from developing countries, often made from recycled or sustainably sourced materials.

Continuing east on Selby Avenue, dining options become more elegant, but one restaurant that is equally accessible is **8** **The Happy Gnome,** a renovated fire station offering more than 40 beers on tap and 100 bottled beers, appetizers, and a full menu for alfresco dining in warm-weather months. After passing Arundel Street, near the end of the block is **9** **Red Cow,** a popular chain serving designer burgers, craft beer, and more.

Continue on Selby Avenue, crossing Western Avenue, where you have a stunning view of the Cathedral of Saint Paul to the east. Here you'll find several opportunities for fine dining. Located in the beautifully restored redbrick-and-sandstone Dacotah Building, **10** **W. A. Frost & Company** serves upscale Mediterranean-influenced fare with an emphasis on locally grown and organic ingredients. This neighborhood institution was mentioned in Jonathan Franzen's novel *Freedom*. Across the street is high-end Russian cuisine at **11** **Moscow on the Hill,** where borscht, caviar, and pelmeni (meat dumplings) are served with an extensive selection of vodka and wine to wash them down.

Summit Overlook Park's bronze eagle originally adorned St. Paul's New York Life building.

Cathedral of Saint Paul

Continue on Selby Avenue past ⓬ **Boyd Park,** named for Frank Boyd, who was instrumental in organizing local railroad porters. Across the street is architect Cass Gilbert's cute little ⓭ **Virginia Street Church** (formerly Swedenborgian Church). This charmer was constructed in 1887 with clapboard, river stones, and shingles.

Turn left on Farrington Street, passing Boyd Park, and turn right on Dayton Avenue. This area is loaded with restored Victorian apartments and condos.

Descend the hill on Dayton Avenue to reach the colossal ⓮ **Cathedral of Saint Paul,** which opened on Palm Sunday in 1915. Designed by Emmanuel Masqueray, the structure was inspired by St. Peter's Basilica in Rome but showcases St. Cloud (Minnesota) granite. It can seat 3,000 parishioners for Mass.

Turn right on Summit Avenue and ascend the hill in the Victorian mansion row to finish the walk. On the left is the ⓯ **James J. Hill House,** the great mansion built by the St. Paul railroad mogul for his 10 children. It is now owned and operated by the Minnesota Historical Society.

Points of Interest

① **Summit Overlook Park** tinyurl.com/summitoverlookpark, 185 Summit Ave., St. Paul, 651-632-5111

② **Minnesota Governor's Residence** mn.gov/admin/governors-residence, 1006 Summit Ave., St. Paul, 651-201-3464

③ **Saint Thomas More Catholic Community** morecommunity.org/parish, 1093 Summit Ave., St. Paul, 651-227-7669

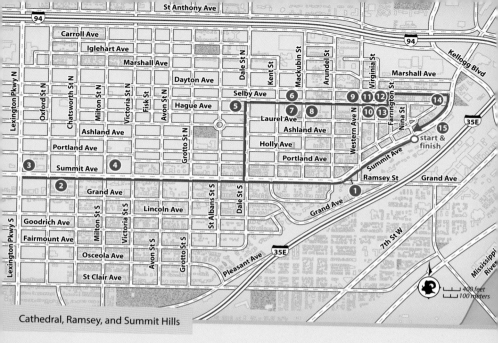

Cathedral, Ramsey, and Summit Hills

4 Mitchell Hamline School of Law mitchellhamline.edu, 875 Summit Ave., St. Paul, 651-227-9171

5 Mississippi Market msmarket.coop, 622 Selby Ave., St. Paul, 651-310-9499

6 Revival revivalfriedchicken.com, 525 Selby Ave., St. Paul, 651-340-2355

7 Ten Thousand Villages tenthousandvillages.com, 520 Selby Ave., St. Paul, 651-225-2043

8 The Happy Gnome thehappygnome.com, 498 Selby Ave., St. Paul, 651-287-2018

9 Red Cow redcowmn.com, 393 Selby Ave., St. Paul, 651-789-0545

10 W. A. Frost & Company wafrost.com, 374 Selby Ave., St. Paul, 651-324-5715

11 Moscow on the Hill moscowonthehill.com, 371 Selby Ave., St. Paul, 651-291-1236

12 Boyd Park stpaul.gov/facilities/boyd-park, 335 Selby Ave., St. Paul, 651-632-5111

13 Virginia Street Church virginiastchurch.org, 170 Virginia St., St. Paul, 651-224-4553

14 Cathedral of Saint Paul cathedralsaintpaul.org, 239 Selby Ave., St. Paul, 651-228-1766

15 James J. Hill House mnhs.org/hillhouse, 240 Summit Ave., St. Paul, 651-297-2555

28 Minnesota State Capitol
Seat of Government Overseeing the Capital City

Above: Minnesota State Capitol

BOUNDARIES: Kellogg Blvd. W., John Ireland Blvd., University Ave., Cedar St.
HUDSON'S TWIN CITIES STREET ATLAS COORDINATES: Map 396, 1D
DISTANCE: About 1.5 miles
DIFFICULTY: Moderate
PARKING: Limited free parking between Park St. and Rice St. on Sherburne St. and Charles St.
PUBLIC TRANSIT: Multiple bus lines to the state capitol; light rail highly recommended

The Minnesota State Capitol, including its adjoining mall, is an architectural masterpiece overlooking scenic downtown St. Paul. The building is situated between downtown and the working-class Frogtown neighborhood, but it is visible for miles. It is one of the state's most beloved architectural landmarks, and for good reason. The current building is the third capitol building in the state's history; its predecessors were destroyed by fire or deemed too small. It is the result of a statewide design competition that was won by 35-year-old St. Paul architect Cass Gilbert in 1895. The masterful, well-proportioned design—glimmering white marble in neoclassical style—belied the architect's young age. However, it went over budget and was not completed until 1905. Legislators complained that the capitol was an extravagant misuse of public funds, but the furor dissipated after it was finished. From the mall you're afforded incredible views of the building's scope, down to its details, including Daniel French and Edward Potter's *Quadriga* (1906)—the elegant horse sculptures at the base of the dome. Plus, don't forget the view of the capitol from the Minnesota History Center, where you can also see an excellent exhibit on Gilbert.

In summer 2017, a more-than-three-year, $309,674,000 renovation of the capitol was finished. It was the building's first renovation since its completion in 1905, repairing crumbling marble and stone and the outdated electrical and plumbing.

Walk Description

Begin on University Avenue and proceed south on Rev. Dr. Martin Luther King Jr. Boulevard, on the west side of the ❶ **Minnesota State Capitol.** If the legislature is in session, politicians and lobbyists are in abundance across from the prosaic State Office Building (1932).

Continue south, crossing the parking lot exit. (The lot is open only for handicapped parking since the renovations.) On the left is a statue of Floyd B. Olson, the Farmer–Labor Party governor who guided the state during the Great Depression and New Deal, only to see his national political aspirations thwarted by terminal cancer in 1936.

Turn right at the crosswalk on Rev. Dr. Martin Luther King Jr. Boulevard, and head south on John Ireland Boulevard. On the mall are numerous statues and memorials. *Roy Wilkins Memorial (Spiral of Justice)* honors the civil rights leader's 46 years of service to the NAACP.

Cross Rice Street/12th Street West. To the left is one of several great views of downtown St. Paul. Turn left on Kellogg Boulevard West. As you descend the hill, you'll come to another scenic vista.

Turn left and follow the sidewalk to the entrance of the ❷ **Minnesota History Center,** home of the Minnesota Historical Society's research libraries, interactive and touring exhibits, and auditorium for films and lectures. It is one of the state's oldest institutions, existing since Minnesota became a territory in 1849. Inside is Market House by D'Amico, an excellent place for coffee, soup, sandwiches, burgers, and daily specials. The restaurant, with a historical flair, pays tribute to the St. Paul "public market," established in 1852.

After exploring the Minnesota Historical Society and its grounds, return to Kellogg Boulevard. Turn right on Kellogg Boulevard and return up the incline, named after Frank B. Kellogg, the state's first elected US Senator (1916) and secretary of state under President Calvin Coolidge. He received the Nobel Peace Prize for the Kellogg-Briand Peace Pact in 1928, when France and the United States, frustrated after the devastation of World War I, attempted to outlaw war through legislation and diplomacy—a utopian policy that was later criticized as politically naive.

Turn right on John Ireland Boulevard, named after the third bishop and first archbishop (1888) of the Roman Catholic Archdiocese of St. Paul and Minneapolis.

After crossing Rice Street/12th Street West, continue straight briefly before turning right on the first sidewalk. Absorb the grandeur of the mall and the capitol to the left. As you approach the Veterans Service Building at the center of the mall, you'll pass numerous war memorials.

Minnesota History Center

Nearby and Notable

The Frogtown neighborhood, part of which (the five blocks between Galtier Street and MacKubin Street) was recently rechristened Little Mekong, is located east of the Minnesota State Capitol. This area is one of the Twin Cities' best areas for delicious, adventurous, and inexpensive dining. University Avenue is lined with a diverse array of ethnic cuisines, especially Southeast Asian, with excellent Vietnamese, Thai, Cambodian, Hmong, and Chinese restaurants for all tastes and pocketbooks. ❹ Ngon offers Vietnamese food in a white-tablecloth atmosphere—outstanding versions of Asian fusion fare are paired with homey standards such as egg roll salad, pho, and a quaffable wine list. ❺ Little Szechuan is a unique choice as the only traditional hot pot restaurant in the Twin Cities. ❻ Cheng Heng Restaurant serves superb, one-of-a-kind Cambodian fare in a relaxed, genuinely "mom, pop, and baby" atmosphere. The menu includes standard Asian items such as fried rice, but the real standouts are the authentic dishes—*chha* mussels, mussels in black bean sauce, and *bánh xèo*, a rice-flour crepe served with pork, shrimp, raw vegetables, and fish sauce. And if that isn't yummy and cheap enough, then head for the astonishing values inside ❼ 88 Oriental Foods deli: a steam table of chicken, beef, and pork stir-fries; soups; and fresh spring rolls at mind-bogglingly low prices—great for a picnic.

At the Veterans Service Building (1954), turn left on one of the two sidewalks that bisect the building and the mall. This symmetrical modern building is situated directly south of the capitol on the mall.

Continue on the parallel sidewalks, passing several Minnesota war memorials. The first is the 2007 World War II Memorial, a recent addition. The oval memorial features 10 glass panels that detail the sacrifices of Minnesotans—more than 320,000 served, 1,250 were prisoners of war, and 6,000 died. Up ahead on the left is the ❸ **Minnesota Vietnam Veterans Memorial** (1992), where the names of the Minnesotans killed or missing in action are inscribed in granite.

Continue on the mall and carefully cross Rev. Dr. Martin Luther King Jr. Boulevard In spring, summer, and early fall, the flower beds here are especially colorful. Walk up the stairs of the capitol and, time permitting, visit its interior and join the insightful Minnesota Historical Society tour.

If you are not going inside the capitol, turn left. Turn right on Rev. Dr. Martin Luther King Jr. Boulevard and follow it to University Avenue to finish the walk.

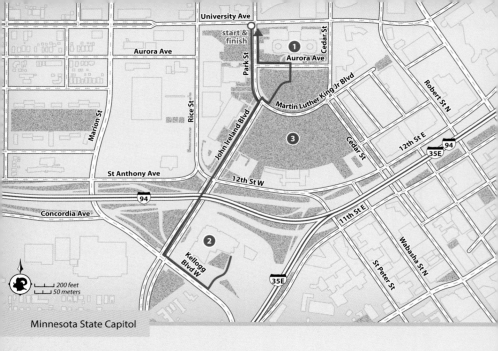

Minnesota State Capitol

Points of Interest

① **Minnesota State Capitol** mnhs.org/capitol, 75 Rev. Dr. Martin Luther King Jr. Blvd., St. Paul, 651-296-2881

② **Minnesota History Center** minnesotahistorycenter.org, 345 Kellogg Blvd. W., St. Paul, 651-259-3900

③ **Minnesota Vietnam Veterans Memorial** mvvm.org, 20 12th St. W., St. Paul, 651-777-0686

④ **Ngon Vietnamese Bistro** ngonbistro.com, 799 University Ave. W., St. Paul, 651-222-3301

⑤ **Little Szechuan Chinese Restaurant and Bar** littleszechuan.com, 422 University Ave. W., St. Paul, 651-222-1333

⑥ **Cheng Heng Restaurant** 448 University Ave. W., St. Paul, 651-222-5577

⑦ **88 Oriental Foods, 291** University Ave. W., St. Paul, 651-209-8388

29 Como Park
St. Paul's Urban Retreat

Above: *Marjorie McNeely Conservatory*

BOUNDARIES: Como Ave., Hamline Ave., Arlington Ave. W., Como Blvd. E., Como Blvd. W.
HUDSON'S TWIN CITIES STREET ATLAS COORDINATES: Map 395, 3B and 4B
DISTANCE: About 2.75 miles
DIFFICULTY: Moderate
PARKING: Como Zoo parking lot; free parking on Horton Ave. and Midway Pkwy.
PUBLIC TRANSIT: Bus lines 3, 61, and 83

Since 1887, Como Park has been a favorite retreat for St. Paul residents and visitors alike. Within its 300-plus acres of parkland are hiking trails, historic bridges and monuments, a free zoo, a restored wooden carousel, an amazing glass-enclosed conservatory, a Japanese garden, multiple butterfly and wildflower gardens, picnic grounds, baseball fields, an amusement park, a pavilion that offers live music during the summer, and, of course, Como Lake. Since the park's opening, the grounds have been worked by some of the finest gardeners in the world, starting in the early 1900s with Itchikawa, landscape gardener for the Mikado of Japan.

Walk Description

In Como Park, start at the front of historic ❶ **Cafesjian's Carousel.** Look for the smallest of the three buildings in the Como Zoo lot—it's the brown wooden one with the horse weather vane mounted on the top, playing loud calliope music during the spring, summer, and early fall months.

Follow the sidewalk along the carousel and take a right at the sidewalk that goes between the parking lot and the new drop-off cul-de-sac.

Take a left to follow Estabrook Drive to the ❷ **Como Park Zoo & Conservatory,** the two large glass buildings after the cul-de-sac. The building with the angular skylights is the entrance to Como Zoo, one of the oldest free zoos in the country. The amazing arabesque glass building ahead of you is the Marjorie McNeely Conservatory, whose gardens got their official start in 1915, when a group of ambitious gardeners planted seeds to grow the first fig and orange trees.

Turn left on Aida Place. All along this walk are native flowers and grasses, as well as exotic flowers and plants. As you approach the conservatory, take a moment to stop and smell the roses—or lilies, or freesias, or whatever else is in bloom in the conservatory's Sunken Garden. The fragrance inside is so powerful that you can smell the flowers through the glass.

Take a right to go past the original entrance of the conservatory, now closed.

Go straight past the conservatory steps and turn right to cross Aida Place. Follow the path through the Monarch Waystation and the Enchanted Garden, where butterfly-attracting plants are grown.

Follow the path to your right to walk beside the Frog Pond, built on the site of the park's first Japanese Garden. Head down to the stairs and go straight.

Turn right, and then make an immediate left. Follow the path to cross the street and pick it up on the other side. Old oak trees are scattered throughout the many picnic areas.

Cross the parking lot and stay on the path. On your left are the ❸ **Como Golf Course and Cross Country Ski Area.** That may sound like a strange combination if you're here in the summer, but spend one winter here and you'll realize what a brilliant idea this multiuse space is.

Follow the serpentine path through the park, and stay left when you come to the first fork. This takes you past a picturesque pond and over the pedestrian bridge that crosses Lexington Parkway North. Up ahead and to your right is Como Lake. The entire park was built with the lake as its focal point, and throughout its history the kidney-shaped lake has been a magnet for bird-watchers, boaters, fishermen, and those out for a romantic stroll. On a more ominous note, when a survey team temporarily drained the lake back in 1923 they found a weighted-down box of human bones. The bones were once believed to belong to James-Younger Gang member Charlie Pitts, whose body had never been recovered after Jesse James and company were gunned down in Northfield, Minnesota. DNA evidence recently proved that the skeleton comes from a yet-unidentified individual who may have died as early as the 1700s.

Turn right after crossing the bridge and follow the path around to the left. The big building up ahead is the ④ **Como Lakeside Pavilion.**

Take your first left to go up to the beautiful, albeit artificial, Hamm Memorial Water Falls. If it's a hot day, this is a wonderful place to stop and cool down.

Head straight and take the first right to go down the hill toward the pavilion. In the summer, you can catch free concerts on the open-air porch out back, including chamber music and performances by local gamelan groups. Inside the building is the ⑤ **Spring Café,** which opened in 2018.

Cross the driveway and keep going straight. Take your first left to follow the lakeshore.

On both sides of the path are native wildflowers and grasses, while on any given summer day egrets, herons, ducks, and Canada geese can be seen on the water.

Stay on the right path (the official pedestrian path) to follow the curve of the lake. Look closely at the cattail and reed thickets you're passing—they're a great place to spot nesting geese and ducks, as well as their hatchlings. On your left is Como Boulevard East, which has an abundance of benches if you need to take a break.

Como Park grounds

When you reach the first parking lot, take the right path around the lot. Then turn left on the gravel path. The rustic, rock-lined pathway takes you just shy of shore level, where you can get a closer look at the wetland flora and fauna. In the spring, this path can get a little swampy, but a little mud on your shoes is well worth the view.

Turn right when you reach asphalt again. On your left is a small pocket of natural wetland that serves as yet another nesting place for waterfowl.

Follow the path uphill to your left, and go straight to follow the contour of the lake. The boxes you see mounted on posts in the lake are for wood ducks. In the wild, wood ducks make their nests up in the trees, and the chicks jump from great heights to bounce on the ground before searching out the nearest body of water. The boxes are a pleasant compromise for city-dwelling wood ducks that must fight squirrels for nesting rights in the trees.

At the next fork, stay on the right path to follow the lake. If you enjoy fishing, the large wooden dock to your right is the place to do it. Nonresidents and residents alike can order a fishing license from the Minnesota Department of Natural Resources (dnr.state.mn.us), which entitles you to fish not only here but also at dozens of other lakes throughout the metro area.

Go straight past the dock and parking lot, and continue following the lakeshore. On your right are old stands of cottonwoods and willows, home to local roosting birds as well as king-fishers and swallows.

At the next fork, take the left path and make a left toward the street. Cross Como Boulevard West and veer left to follow Horton Avenue. Follow the sidewalk along the stone retaining wall.

Cross Churchill Street and go straight. Just before you get to Lexington Parkway North, turn right and follow the left fork to head down the path. From here, you can get a closer look at the historic **6 Como Streetcar Station.** The station has limited visiting hours, but you can walk around the grounds to view the exterior and the former streetcar bridge just behind it.

Take the left fork and follow the path west. Take your first left to follow the path under the bridge. From here, you can get a good picture of where the old streetcar line used to run. Go straight and follow the path to the left. At the fork, take the left path and continue following it to the right. Turn right at the fork and go straight, heading northwest. On your right is a big picnic area; the large pavilion up ahead has restrooms, drinking fountains, and additional picnic tables.

Go straight across the parking lot entrance, and follow the path along Horton Avenue. At Midway Parkway, turn right. Go straight to cross the parking lot entrance, and go straight past the fork. Follow the path up the hill and through the woods. At the street crossing, look ahead and to the right. The big brown building with the horse weather vane on top is Cafesjian's Carousel, which is where we started.

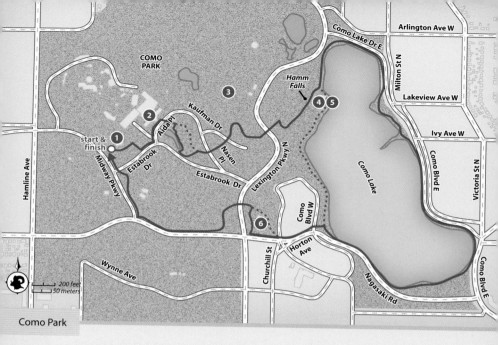

Como Park

Points of Interest

1 **Cafesjian's Carousel** ourfaircarousel.org, 1245 Midway Pkwy., St. Paul, 651-489-4628

2 **Como Park Zoo & Conservatory** comozooconservatory.org, 1225 Estabrook Dr., St. Paul, 651-487-8200

3 **Como Golf Course and Cross Country Ski Area** stpaul.golf/como-gc or tinyurl.com/comoskiing, 1431 Lexington Pkwy. N., St. Paul, 651-488-9673

4 **Como Lakeside Pavilion** tinyurl.com/comolakesidepavilion, 1360 Lexington Pkwy. N., St. Paul, 651-488-4920

5 **Spring Café** springcafestp.com, 1360 Lexington Pkwy. N., St. Paul

6 **Como Streetcar Station** tinyurl.com/streetcarstation, 1224 Lexington Pkwy. N., St. Paul, 651-632-5111

30 Irvine Park and West Seventh Street

Where the Oldest Neighborhood Meets the Newest Place to Play

Above: *The Science Museum of Minnesota*

BOUNDARIES: Shepard Rd., Seventh St. W., Kellogg Blvd. W., Irvine Park
HUDSON'S TWIN CITIES STREET ATLAS COORDINATES: Map 396, 1D; Map 423, 1A
DISTANCE: About 1.5 miles
DIFFICULTY: Moderate
PARKING: Limited 2-hour parking on Exchange St.
PUBLIC TRANSIT: Bus lines 3, 21, 54, 63, and 74

This walk juxtaposes St. Paul's oldest surviving neighborhood, Irvine Park, with the newest hot spot where St. Paul goes to party, West Seventh Street. Historically, the West Seventh Street neighborhood was a hardscrabble, working-class, and close-knit community largely from two villages in southern Italy. The Italian immigrants made the most of the often-flooded Upper later known as Little Italy. They were relocated by the city after 1960—Cossetta is one of the surviving businesses that moved up the hill from the levee, where Shepard Road and upscale condos are now located. Since Xcel Energy Center opened in 2000, the area has become a bustling business district filled with restaurants and bars that are popular venues for celebrating after Minnesota Wild hockey games, concerts, conventions, and events.

In contrast, Irvine Park provides several examples of the state's history and fine architecture in a neighborhood that has been on the National Register of Historic Places since 1973. Plotted in 1849, the homes comprise a collection of types—restorations, those moved to the site, and recent infill construction. Enjoy the historic homes, then sit down for a nosh and a drink, or an elegant meal and a bottle of wine.

Walk Description

Begin at the corner of Walnut Street and Exchange Street South, and walk southeast down Walnut Street. On the right is ❶ **Forepaugh's Restaurant,** serving upscale continental cuisine in an immense three-story Victorian mansion with a mansard roof (1870). It was once the home of a prominent dry-goods seller, Joseph Forepaugh, his wife, and two daughters. Shortly after moving in, he was caught having an affair with their maid, Molly, who soon after committed suicide. Today, the house is said to be haunted by entities of Molly and Joseph, who regularly appear as apparitions, turn the lights on and off, and make strange noises.

Cross the intersection at ❷ **Irvine Park** and turn right on the sidewalk in the beautiful urban park, which started as a grazing area for horses in 1849 but has since been modified to its present splendor.

At the corner of the park, turn left. Across the street are several historic homes. On the corner is the only Gothic Revival home in the neighborhood, the Jay and Henry Knox House (26 Irvine Park). Another beauty is the Parker-Marshall House (30 Irvine Park), built in 1852. It was at one time the home of William Marshall, who served as governor of Minnesota from 1866 to 1870. The house has been moved several times—in both cases, only a few addresses down from its original location at 35 Irvine Park—as have several other homes in the area, including the Federal-style Simpson-Wood House, which was moved to 32 Irvine Park from nearby Sherman Street.

Cross Ryan Avenue and continue following the sidewalk in the park. Across the street is the Murray-Lanpher House (35 Irvine Park), an enormous Queen Anne from 1886. The Wagner-Marty House (38 Irvine Park) is a Greek Revival–style mansion that began its life in the 1850s in suburban Woodbury and now sits on the site of at least three previous homes.

Turn left on Irvine Park. Among the many striking mansions on Walnut Street, the classical grandeur of the Wright-Pendergast House (233 Walnut St.) stands out. The house was originally constructed in Greek Revival style in 1851 but was substantially modified in 1907 with the addition of an immense neoclassical portico and Ionic pediment. On the corner is the Italianate John McDonald House (56 Irvine Park), constructed in 1873 and now turned into condominiums.

Turn left on Irvine Park. Across the street is the Dr. Justus Ohage House (59 Irvine Park). The Romanesque Revival mansion was built in 1889 for the man responsible for creating St. Paul's public health system.

Turn right on Ryan Avenue. Constructed in 1851, the Humphrey-Willis House (240 Ryan Ave.) is unusual for the neighborhood because of its cottage size, but it is quite elegant in its symmetrical Georgian style. Next door, the Charles Symonds House (234 Ryan Ave.), a simple structure built in 1850, is the oldest in St. Paul.

Turn right on the one-way street that intersects Eagle Parkway up the hill. Just before the railroad tracks is the Armstrong-Quinlan House, a double house that was built in 1886 as a rental

Alexander Ramsey House

property and later used as a nursing home. It was originally located on Fifth Street in a vast parking lot across from the Xcel Energy Center, where it sat vacant for years. After countless studies and plans for its renovation, it was moved in 2001 for $2 million to its current site and converted to condos.

Go straight ahead, heading southeast, and cross Shepard Road. Turn left on Shepard Road on the path along the Mississippi River. From here, several paths lead to the water, park benches, and sculptures. Turn left on Ontario Street, carefully crossing the railroad tracks, and follow the sidewalk along the perimeter of the Science Museum's Big Back Yard.

Ascend the steps to the left until you reach the first level, then continue straight ahead. Above is the ❸ **Science Museum of Minnesota,** founded in 1907, though in a different location. The 370,000-square-foot building, including one temporary gallery and five permanent galleries, opened in 1999 on this beautiful site overlooking the Mississippi River. Inside the museum, the U.S. Department of the Interior runs the helpful ❹ **Mississippi National River and Recreation Center.**

Cross the metal bridge. The Big Back Yard has combined a selection of native Minnesota trees, flowers, and grasses. Numerous markers provide information on the flora and its relationship to various natural biomes in the state and region. Follow the path as it veers right at the intersection after passing the Science House, a resource center for students and teachers that was constructed with state-of-the-art environmental technology. Follow the sidewalk on the outside perimeter of the park closest to the Science Museum.

Cross Eagle Parkway and turn right to cross Chestnut Street. On the corner is *Charlie Andiamo Americano,* a sculpted tribute to St. Paul–born and –raised *Peanuts* cartoonist Charles Schulz and to the families who settled the Upper Levee. Up the steep hill is the ❺ **Xcel Energy Center** ("the X"), which was completed in 2000. Home of the National Hockey League's Minnesota Wild, the building also hosts concerts and conventions, including the 2008 Republican National Convention. There's additional event space in the adjoining River Centre and Roy Wilkins Auditorium, the cozier venue named in honor of the great civil rights leader.

Continue straight across West Seventh Street and immediately turn left to follow Seventh Street. This is the West Seventh Street business district, where St. Paul celebrates after sporting events at the X. On the right is ❻ **The Liffey Irish Pub.** This drinking establishment is the real McCoy, where a properly poured Guinness can be quaffed with appetizers or dinner on a comely terrace in warm weather. Just ahead is ❼ **Cossetta Alimentari**—"a taste of the levee," as it advertises—where St. Paul's first Italian community was located and later forcibly relocated when the levee was declared unsafe for habitation. The recently renovated and expanded restaurant has the best old-school Little Italy–style cuisine in colossal proportions. Grab a workman-size slab of

Alexander Ramsey: Pioneer Politician

Alexander Ramsey was the first great politician in Minnesota. His impact is still felt today in the state's borders and in his namesake county that's home to the capital. Like most early political and business leaders, his origins were outside the state; he arrived from Pennsylvania after President Zachary Taylor named him territorial governor. Ramsey was a Whig, and later a nascent Republican, in a territory dominated by Democrats. His early career as a politician in Minnesota was controversial at best: His appointment by Washington, D.C., to negotiate with the Dakota Indians culminated in the treaty of 1851, in which the Dakota ceded vast lands to the area that became Minnesota, for minimal money. Resentment over the deal led in part to the Dakota Conflict of 1862. Later, as a US senator voicing a strong belief in Manifest Destiny, he called for annexing Rupert's Land, fur-trade areas in central and western Canada. However, after the Civil War, in the era of the Reconstruction, there was little enthusiasm for pursuing his expansionist interests, and the state's original 1858 border remained.

The Minnesota Historical Society focuses on another side of Ramsey—his family life in the 1870s, during St. Paul's Victorian era. His home in the Irvine Park neighborhood includes exquisite marble furnaces and walnut woodwork, as well as about 95% of the original furnishings.

pizza and appreciate the wall-to-wall photos from the heyday of the levee. Upstairs is its upscale restaurant, Louis Ristorante & Bar.

Cross Chestnut Street. On the right is ❽ **Patrick McGovern's Pub & Restaurant,** a charming Irish bar for more than 20 years. Across the street is ❾ **Tom Reid's Hockey City Pub,** named after the former Minnesota North Star hockey player and announcer. It's a favorite hangout for watching hockey games on the big-screen televisions and for drinking cheap beer.

After crossing Walnut Street, turn left to cross West Seventh Street, and continue on Walnut Street toward the Irvine Park neighborhood.

Turn right on Exchange Street South to finish the walk. At 265 Exchange St. South is the ❿ **Alexander Ramsey House,** a lovely French Second Empire mansion built in 1872 for Minnesota's first territorial governor and second state governor.

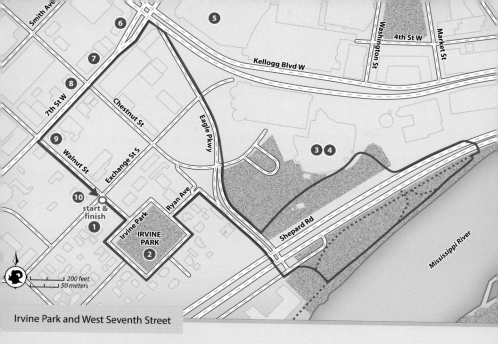

Irvine Park and West Seventh Street

Points of Interest

1. **Forepaugh's Restaurant** forepaughs.com, 276 Exchange St. S., St. Paul, 651-224-5606

2. **Irvine Park** tinyurl.com/irvineparkmn, 251 Walnut St., St. Paul, 651-632-5111

3. **Science Museum of Minnesota** smm.org, 120 Kellogg Blvd. W., St. Paul, 651-221-9444

4. **Mississippi National River and Recreation Area** nps.gov/miss, 120 Kellogg Blvd. W., St. Paul, 651-292-0200

5. **Xcel Energy Center** xcelenergycenter.com, 175 Kellogg Blvd. W., St. Paul, 651-265-4800

6. **The Liffey Irish Pub** theliffey.com, 175 7th St. W., St. Paul, 651-556-1420

7. **Cossetta Alimentari/Louis Ristorante & Bar** cossettas.com, 211 7th St. W., St. Paul, 651-222-3476

8. **Patrick McGovern's Pub & Restaurant** patmcgoverns.com, 225 7th St. W., St. Paul, 651-224-5821

9. **Tom Reid's Hockey City Pub** tomreids.com, 258 7th St. W., St. Paul, 651-292-9916

10. **Alexander Ramsey House** mnhs.org/ramseyhouse, 265 Exchange St. S., St. Paul, 651-296-8760

31 Downtown St. Paul
Mears Park to Rice Park

Above: *The Art Deco–style Mickey's Dining Car*

BOUNDARIES: Fifth St. W., Washington St., Seventh St. W., Wacouta St.
HUDSON'S TWIN CITIES STREET ATLAS COORDINATES: Map 396, 1D
DISTANCE: About 2 miles
DIFFICULTY: Easy
PARKING: 2-hour metered parking near Mears Park, on Fifth St., Sixth St., and Wacouta St.
PUBLIC TRANSIT: Numerous bus lines to Mears Park

Former Minnesota governor Jesse Ventura once caused a near scandal by stating on the *Late Show with David Letterman* that St. Paul's streets were laid out by drunk Irishmen—a claim that visitors driving in the area have been more than happy to agree with. However, we think that the following St. Paul walk, starting at Mears Park and looping past Rice Park, might reveal a little bit of the genius in the madness. The angles of the streets and sidewalks give pedestrians the best possible view of the architecture, from the ornate buildings in Lowertown to the historic cultural centers that encircle Rice Park. In recent years, Lowertown has blossomed into a hot outpost for restaurants, nightlife, and new condos. In the winter, this area comes alive with Winter Carnival events, from subzero parades to sparkling ice sculptures; during the rest of the year, the streets are lined with flowers and perfectly manicured trees.

Walk Description

Start at ❶ **Mears Park,** where the Twin Cities Jazz Festival is annually held. At the corner of Sixth Street East and Sibley Street, cross Sibley Street, going southwest, and turn left at Sibley to get to the ❷ **Cray Plaza** entrance on Sibley Street across from Mears Park.

Enter Cray Plaza, formerly named Galtier Plaza after Father Lucien Galtier, the Catholic priest who, in 1841, changed the name of the small settlement of Pig's Eye to Saint Paul's Landing, which was later shortened to St. Paul.

Take the escalator up to the second floor and turn right to go around the top of the escalator and head straight down the hall. As you're walking, you'll see the old Galtier movie theater marquee suspended against the wall to your right. The movie theater has long been closed, but the marquee is kept brightly lit nonetheless.

Enter the 375 Jackson skyway at the end of the building and go straight. This skyway offers a view of St. Paul's Lowertown outskirts. On your left you can see the former First National Bank Building—the gigantic red "1" prominently displayed on top of the building makes a handy landmark for navigating downtown St. Paul.

Go through the next skyway to enter the First National Bank/U.S. Bank Building. Take the second right to walk alongside the marble wall at the end of the walkway. Follow the path around to the Fifth Street Center/Minnesota Street skyway entrance.

Go through the skyway to the Alliance Bank Center. Take the left path and go straight. Just before the escalators, turn right to enter the Town Square/Sixth Street skyway and go straight.

Follow the path to your right and make a left at the dining court. Here you'll find ❸ **La Loma Tamales,** which makes its tamales from scratch, including grinding its own corn for the masa dough. Turn left again and walk toward Macy's (follow the overhead directional signs). Go straight into the Wells Fargo Place building.

Turn right at the ATM and go to the left of the escalator and into the Wells Fargo atrium.

Turn left to exit the building onto Wabasha Street North. Across the street is the ❹ **Palace Theatre,** the only vaudeville house in St. Paul that was not demolished. Charlie Chaplin, George

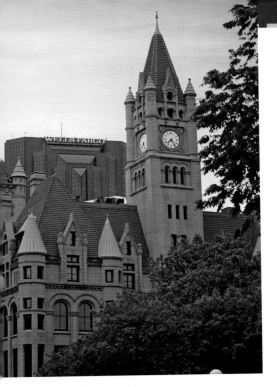
Landmark Center

Burns, and the Marx Brothers all appeared on the Palace's stage during its heyday. First Avenue and JAM Productions have recently partnered to bring new live music events to the classic space. Cross the street and turn right to follow Wabasha Street past neighborhood favorite ❺ **Candyland,** which has been in this location since 1932. Don't miss the delicious warm gummi bears. Down the street you can see the back of ❻ **The Fitzgerald Theater,** St. Paul's oldest theater and the original home of the radio show *A Prairie Home Companion.*

Turn left at West Seventh Street to pass the ❼ **Minnesota Children's Museum,** which reopened in summer of 2017 after a $30 million expansion and renovation to feature all-new exhibits. Go straight to the corner. Across the street from here, you'll see the distinctive Art Deco ❽ **Mickey's Dining Car,** which has appeared in such movies as *The Mighty Ducks I, II,* and *III; Jingle All the Way;* and *A Prairie Home Companion.* Across the street is ❾ **Church of the Assumption,** built in 1874.

Turn left on St. Peter Street. At 444 and 448 St. Peter St. are the former Coney Island Restaurant buildings—number 448 is the oldest building in St. Paul still located on its original site, constructed in 1858 as the state arsenal.

Turn right at the Seventh Place Arch, going south to follow Washington Street/Ecolab Place past the impressive Romanesque/Châteauesque–style ❿ **Landmark Center.** The center was built in 1902 and originally served as the federal courthouse and a post office. Now a cultural center for the area, it was once the site of notable St. Paul gangster trials, including the one held for Alvin "Creepy" Karpis.

Cross West Fifth Street and then cross Washington Street/Ecolab Place into ⓫ **Rice Park.** Originally plotted in 1849 by the early developers of St. Paul, this park is the site of the first electric streetlights in St. Paul, installed to celebrate the completion of the Northern Pacific Railroad's line to the West Coast.

Surrounding the park are some of the most impressive downtown St. Paul historic buildings, including the opulent St. Paul Hotel, the **12 Ordway Center for the Performing Arts,** the **13 George Latimer Central Library,** the **14 James J. Hill Center.**

After you've explored the park, continue to the corner of West Fifth Street and Market Street, and turn left. Walk past Landmark Center and go straight across Sixth Street. Turn right into the Seventh Place Arch and go straight through the courtyard.

Enter the Wells Fargo building at 430 Wabasha St. N.; go straight. Take the first left and make a right at the overlook.

Turn left into the Town Square building and go straight. Turn right at the dining court and take the right path just before the escalator. Enter the skyway to Alliance Bank Center and follow the path to the left. Turn left at the escalators and go straight through to the skyway exit.

Enter the U.S. Bank Building and take the path to your left. Follow the path to the U.S. Bank Center sign, and then take the left path to the 375 Jackson Building.

Enter the skyway to the 375 Jackson Building. Go straight into the next skyway and then into Galtier Plaza. Go straight past the escalators and all the way to the big bank of windows on the other side of the building. Take the escalator down to the dining court. Turn right at the bottom of the escalator, go down the hall, and exit the building. Turn left to head toward the corner of East Sixth and Sibley Streets.

Turn right and cross the street to Mears Park, where you started. Across the street is **15 Barrio,** an extraordinary Mexican restaurant and tequila bar with items such as soft-shell crab and mahimahi tacos.

Church of the Assumption

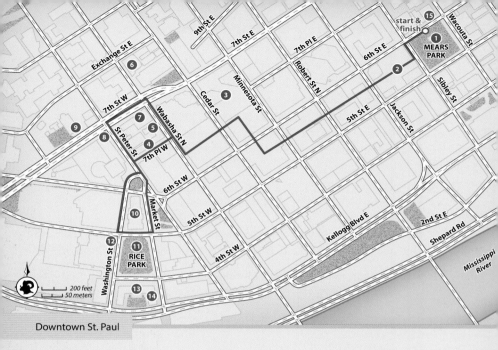

Downtown St. Paul

Points of Interest

1. **Mears Park** tinyurl.com/mearspark, 221 5th St. E., St. Paul, 651-632-5111
2. **Cray Plaza** crayplazastpaul.com, 380 Jackson St., St. Paul
3. **La Loma Tamales** laloma.com, 444 Cedar St., Ste. 210, St. Paul, 651-202-3153
4. **Palace Theatre** palacestpaul.com, 17 7th Pl. W., St. Paul, 651-338-8388
5. **Candyland** candylandstore.com, 435 Wabasha St. N., St. Paul, 651-292-1191
6. **The Fitzgerald Theater** fitzgeraldtheater.publicradio.org, 10 Exchange St. E., St. Paul, 651-290-1200
7. **Minnesota Children's Museum** mcm.org, 10 7th St. W., St. Paul, 651-225-6000
8. **Mickey's Dining Car** mickeysdiningcar.com, 36 7th St. W., St. Paul, 651-698-0259
9. **Church of the Assumption** assumptionsp.org, 51 7th St. W., St. Paul, 651-224-7536
10. **Landmark Center** landmarkcenter.org, 75 5th St. W., St. Paul, 651-292-3225
11. **Rice Park** stpaul.gov/facilities/rice-park, 109 4th St. W., St. Paul, 651-266-6400
12. **Ordway Center for the Performing Arts** ordway.org, 345 Washington St., St. Paul, 651-282-3000
13. **George Latimer Public Library** tinyurl.com/stpaulcentrallibrary, 90 4th St. W., St. Paul, 651-266-7000
14. **James J. Hill Center** jjhill.org, 80 4th St. W., St. Paul, 651-265-5500
15. **Barrio** barriotequila.com, 235 6th St. E., St. Paul, 651-222-3250

32 West Side
Ethnic Past Meets Ethnic Renaissance

Above: Colorado Street Bridge

BOUNDARIES: Cesar Chavez St., Ada St., Clinton Ave./Robie St. E., Delos St. E.
HUDSON'S TWIN CITIES STREET ATLAS COORDINATES: Map 423, 2A
DISTANCE: About 1 mile
DIFFICULTY: Easy
PARKING: Free parking on Congress St. and Clinton Ave.
PUBLIC TRANSIT: Bus lines 62, 67, 68, and 75

Directly south of downtown St. Paul and across the Mississippi River, the West Side is a geographic misnomer and an interesting historical and present-day neighborhood. It was settled after the first Wabasha Street Bridge was completed in 1859 but was not annexed by the city until 1874. The river was then a filthy industrial area prone to flooding, so, not surprisingly, the West Side was settled by a mix of poor ethnic groups. The Jewish community accounted for more than 70% of the neighborhood's population in 1915. Once significantly larger as the West Side Flats, the size of the business and residential area was reduced by urban renewal and later transformed into an industrial park.

In recent years, the area has become St. Paul's largest Chicano business district, known as the District del Sol. St. Michael's Catholic Church, originally an Italian congregation, became the Torre de San Miguel Homes in 1968. A few years earlier, the Frias family opened Boca Chica, the still-thriving Mexican restaurant. More recently, Concord Avenue was renamed Cesar Chavez Street. The area is layered with ethnic history, which continues through the bilingual businesses today. The neighborhood has played a pivotal role in St. Paul's history, and its prime location suggests that it will continue to do so.

Walk Description

Start on the corner of Isabel Street East and Clinton Avenue, and walk north on Clinton Avenue. On the left are the gorgeous Isabel Apartments (109–119 Isabel St. E.). The row houses were constructed in 1904 in front of an immense old cottonwood tree that stands behind the building.

Turn left on the pedestrian path and then continue west on Delos Street East. The bridge crosses Robert Street South and provides a panoramic view of the St. Paul skyline to the north. After crossing the bridge, you'll come to the Torre de San Miguel Homes, a housing project from

El Burrito Mercado, a Mexican American market, restaurant, and deli

the late 1960s that has undergone several renovations. It's home to a diverse group of immigrants from all over the world, most notably Mexico, Somalia, and Laos.

Turn left on Livingston Avenue at the cul-de-sac, and then immediately turn right on Delos Street to continue west. On the right is the Torre de San Miguel, once the tower for St. Michael's Catholic Church, an Italian church built in 1882. The tower is the oldest remaining piece of architecture from the historic West Side Flats neighborhood.

Continue, walking up the steps. On the right is the Colorado Street Bridge, built in 1888. It has served as a pedestrian bridge for a number of years. If you'd like a historic lager or a fun taproom experience, turn right. Ahead is ❶ **The Yoerg Saloon,** serving beer, wine, and German-inspired food. The rebuilt former Wabasha Bar features a version of Anthony Yoerg's 1848 steam beer, lagered in the Bavarian tradition, originally in caves along downtown St. Paul. Next door, in contrast, is ❷ **Wabasha Brewing Company,** a former bar turned taproom with a nice patio and a quarterly art wall showcasing local artists.

Turn left, southeast, on Cesar Chavez Street. This is the heart of the District del Sol. ❸ **Boca Chica** has served an enormous menu of standard Mexican fare since 1964. The restaurant has grown over the years with the economic and cultural reemergence of the West Side.

Cross Robert Street South, an intersection filled with Mexican American businesses and, toward the hill, a colorful sun mural. Ahead on the left is ❹ **Parque de Castillo,** a neighborhood park that hosts a summer music-and-movies series.

Cross State Street to follow Cesar Chavez Street. On the left is ❺ **El Burrito Mercado,** established in 1979. The Mexican American market, restaurant (El Café Restaurant), and deli predated the emergence of the West Side Chicano community. It offers reasonably priced, authentic Mexican food, such as tamales, tacos, chicken mole, homemade salsas, a wide selection of imported Mexican cheeses, fresh meats and seafood, and myriad other items.

Turn left on Ada Street. Continue across Robie Street East and turn left. On the right is the ❺ **Paul and Sheila Wellstone Center for Community.** Completed in 2006, the center was named in honor of Minnesota's Democratic senator Paul Wellstone and his wife, Sheila, who both died in a plane crash in 2002. It serves as a meeting and event venue and as the headquarters for Neighborhood House, founded by Mount Zion Temple for Russian Jewish immigrants in 1897. The organization now serves immigrants, refugees, and low-income populations. If the building is open, you are invited to view the public art displayed inside.

After passing the multilingual murals on the Wellstone Center, Robie Street East merges into Clinton Avenue. Continue north to pass Parque de Castillo. Finish the walk at the intersection of Isabel Street East.

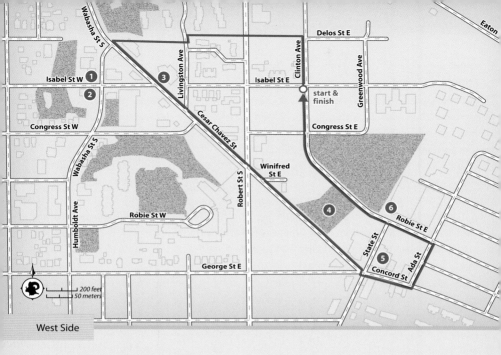

Points of Interest

1. **The Yoerg Saloon** yoergbeer.com/the_yoerg_pub, 427 Wabasha St. S., St. Paul, 763-200-3645

2. **Wabasha Brewing Company** wabashabrewing.com, 429 Wabasha St. S., St. Paul, 651-224-2102

3. **Boca Chica Restaurante Mexicano & Cantina** bocachicarestaurant.com, 11 Cesar Chavez St., St. Paul, 651-222-8499

4. **Parque de Castillo** stpaul.gov/facilities/parque-de-castillo, 149 Cesar Chavez St., St. Paul, 651-632-5111

5. **El Burrito Mercado** elburritomercado.com, 175 Cesar Chavez St., St. Paul, 651-291-0758

6. **Paul and Sheila Wellstone Center for Community** neighb.org, 179 Robie St. E., St. Paul, 651-789-2500

33 Swede Hollow/Dayton's Bluff
The Working Class Moves Up to the Bluffs

Above: *Seventh Street Improvement Arches, constructed using the helicoidal method*

BOUNDARIES: Sixth St. E., Payne Ave., Minnehaha Ave. E., Arcade St.
HUDSON'S TWIN CITIES STREET ATLAS COORDINATES: Map 396, 2C and 2D
DISTANCE: About 2 miles
DIFFICULTY: Moderate
PARKING: Parking lots on Payne Ave. and Seventh St. E.
PUBLIC TRANSIT: Bus lines 70 and 74

Long before building codes and neighborhood zoning laws, Swedish immigrants first settled in what was then a marginal, flood-prone piece of land east of downtown St. Paul, in a small valley they called Svenska Dalen. For more than 100 years, Swede Hollow, as it became known, was home to thousands of poor immigrant families living in essentially slum conditions—first Swedes, then Italians, and, in the last days of Swede Hollow, Mexicans—until the city condemned the area in the urban renewal of the 1950s.

Although the hundreds of houses that once filled Swede Hollow are gone, you'll occasionally see a squared cluster of bricks that marks where a house once stood. All along the upper cliffs of the area stand successful businesses started by former residents—most notably James Morelli, whose descendants still own the wonderful Morelli's Italian deli and liquor store, and Gentille Yarusso, whose descendants own Yarusso-Bros. Italian Restaurant.

Walk Description

At Payne Avenue and East Seventh Street, enter the curlicue of the Bruce Vento Trailhead, and follow the path down to the first fork, into ❶ **Swede Hollow Park.** Make a left at the bottom of the hill and follow the path under the set of picturesque stone bridges directly ahead—the Seventh Street Improvement Arches. These bridges, built in 1884, are the only known examples in Minnesota of bridges constructed according to the helicoidal, or spiral method; only a few other examples exist elsewhere in the United States.

St. Paul's Flat Earth brewery

Follow the path through the woods. On your right is Phalen Creek, home to many native species of birds, including ducks, egrets, herons, and Canada geese. At the first green bench, notice the steps leading to the creek on your right. The valley below you is the former site of the Swede Hollow community. Scant evidence of it remains along the creek, but it's worth your while to go down the steps to investigate.

Continue along the Bruce Vento Trail. At the first fork in the trail—look for the PAYNE AVENUE BUSINESS DISTRICT signpost on your right—turn left to go under the white bridge. This path will take you up to street level. This white tunnel is the only road in or out of Swede Hollow.

Head up the hill and turn right at the SWEDE HOLLOW PARK sign. Follow the alley to Payne Avenue. Go right on Payne and continue north. Turn right when you get to

Edward Phelan: Notorious Early Settler

Edward Phelan (whose name was variously spelled Phalen and Felyn) was a landowner who affixed his name to many pieces of property around his cabin, including Lake Phalen and Phalen Creek. Phelan was also the first person in St. Paul to be accused of murder, after his business partner, John Hays, was killed in 1839. Phelan himself was killed by his traveling companions in "self-defense" when he fled the state to evade prosecution. Local historian John Fletcher Williams wrote in 1876: "It is a disgrace, that the name of this brutal murderer has been affixed to one of our most beautiful lakes."

Minnehaha Avenue East to walk past the amazing old Hamm's Brewery fortress at 690 Minnehaha Ave. E. If you're over 40, you might remember seeing the Hamm's Bear beer commercials when you were a kid. The commercials are now shown for camp effect in art theaters and at film festivals. ❷ **St. Paul's Flat Earth** brewery relocated to this beautifully renovated space. Also within the old Hamm's complex are Urban Organics, an aquaponics company, and Eleven Wells Spirits distillery, maker of rum and whiskey, including a re-creation of the historic Minnesota 13 white whiskey.

Continue on Minnehaha. About two blocks ahead is the site of the 1951 3M explosion, which killed 15 and injured 50. In recent years, 3M's historic industrial plant exited the city of St. Paul.

Turn right on Arcade Street and go straight (south). If you like authentic Mexican food, ❸ **Taqueria Los Paisanos** has excellent fare, including reasonably priced seafood. Across the street, ❹ **Mañana Restaurante y Pupuseria** is the place for Salvadoran food, such as homemade empanadas and wonderful corn *pupusas,* the national dish of El Salvador.

Turn right to head southwest on East Seventh Street. Turn right at the Mexican Consulate building at the corner of Sinnen Street and East Seventh Street, and go west down Margaret Street East to ❺ **Hamm Park.** This park is the former site of the Hamm Mansion, home of Theodore and Louisa Buchholz Hamm, who started the Hamm Brewing Company in 1865. At the far left corner of the park, you'll find a set of stairs. Take the stairs down to Bates Avenue.

Turn right to go straight on Bates Avenue, past the stop sign and through the little neighborhood park at North Street East and Bates Avenue. At the left side of the park is ❻ **Swede Hollow Cafe,** a great stop for a cup of coffee and a bite to eat. Or continue walking, and on the right is ❼ **The Goat Coffeehouse,** which offers coffee and food, as well as art.

Turn right on East Seventh Street, heading southwest. Continue to Mounds Boulevard. Cross the street and continue until you reach Payne Avenue. Turn left into the parking lot.

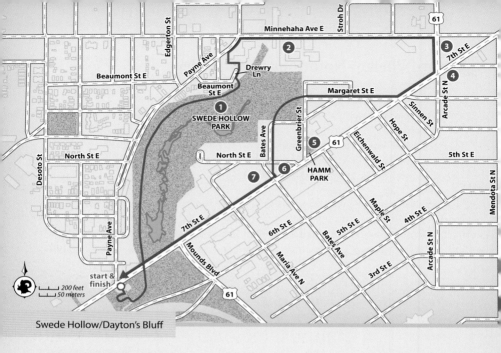

Points of Interest

1. **Swede Hollow Park** swedehollow.org or tinyurl.com/swedehollow, 615 7th St. E., St. Paul, 651-632-5111

2. **St. Paul's Flat Earth** flatearthbrewing.com, 688 Minnehaha Ave. E., St. Paul, 651-698-1945

3. **Taqueria Los Paisanos** lospaisanostaqueria.com, 825 7th St. E., St. Paul, 651-778-8062

4. **Mañana Restaurante y Pupuseria** saintpaulrestaurant.com, 828 7th St. E., St. Paul, 651-793-8482

5. **Hamm Park** tinyurl.com/hammpark, 743 7th St. E., St. Paul, 651-632-5111

6. **Swede Hollow Cafe** swedehollowcafe.com, 725 7th St. E., St. Paul, 651-776-8810

7. **The Goat Coffeehouse** goatcoffeehouse.com, 699 7th St. E., St. Paul, 651-200-4370

34 Indian Mounds Regional Park/Bruce Vento Nature Sanctuary Nature, Cityscapes, and History

Above: Burial mounds at Indian Mounds Regional Park

BOUNDARIES: Warner Rd., Fourth St. E., Mounds Blvd., Clermont St.
HUDSON'S TWIN CITIES STREET ATLAS COORDINATES: Map 396, 3D
DISTANCE: About 4 miles
DIFFICULTY: Strenuous
PARKING: Free parking in the Indian Mounds Regional Park parking lot, located at Cherry St. and Mounds Blvd.
PUBLIC TRANSIT: Bus lines 70 and 74

Established in 1893, Indian Mounds Regional Park is one of the oldest parks in St. Paul. The park's name comes from the American Indian burial mounds that were found here by early settlers. These included 2,000-year-old Hopewell mounds, while others were constructed by the Dakota much later. Originally, there were 36 mounds in the park, but because of shortsighted construction projects and vandalism, only 6 remain.

At the northwest corner is the Bruce Vento Nature Sanctuary, the newest addition to the park. In the sanctuary, you'll be treated to sights of native birds and prairie grass, the previously inaccessible Carver's Cave and Brewer's Cave, and close-up views of freight trains rumbling down the same rails they've traversed for nearly 100 years. Pack a lunch—you won't find anywhere to buy food along this route, but you will find plenty of scenic places to stop and have a picnic. For more in-depth background on the park and its fascinating history, give a ranger a call at 877-727-1172, ext. 11, to listen to a recording about the area.

Walk Description

Begin at the Indian Mounds Regional Park parking lot, located at Cherry Street and Mounds Boulevard. Follow the sidewalk to your right, facing the overlook. From here, you have a scenic view of downtown St. Paul; the state capitol; the Roberts, Wabasha, and High Bridges; the curve of the Mississippi River; and old railway beds.

Turn left, northwest, at the corner of Mounds Boulevard and Plum Street onto the walking path. Follow the path downhill to parallel Commercial Street. At the stop sign at the bottom of the hill, cross the street at East Fourth Street and Commercial Street. Following the curve of the park entrance, go straight down East Fourth Street and make your first left into the ❶ **Bruce Vento Nature Sanctuary** parking lot.

Go straight through the short parking lot and onto the sanctuary trail. The sanctuary is home to many common and uncommon native birds, including bald eagles, northern flickers, great blue herons, and red-tailed hawks. Native species of flora are also planted here on these grounds, a project maintained by Minnesota's East Side Youth Conservation Corps. At the trailhead, informative markers provide the history of the area, as well as bird-identification guides for bird-watchers.

Go straight past the first fork in the path as it curves northeast. Occasionally, trains rumble past this area, and the trail offers lots of places to catch a closer look at them.

Stay on the path closest to the bluffs as it moves southeast, and head up the bluffs to the oak woodland restoration area. Many lovely old trees—both dead and alive, and home to downy woodpeckers and other birds—are found along this part of the path. New trees have been planted here with the hope that someday this will resemble, once again, the oak forest as it was before the railways came through.

Continue southeast. Just past the fork and on your left is Brewer's Cave, which, if you're a beer connoisseur, you might recognize from the picture on the Brewer's Cave Beer label. The pure stream coming from the rocks maintains a fairly constant temperature year-round, meaning this

Turtle sunning at Bruce Vento Nature Sanctuary

fount is one of the first places where you'll see new growth in the early days of spring. The little creek empties over a tiny, picturesque waterfall and into a nice-size pond—home to nesting waterbirds, including Canada geese, wood ducks, and mallards, and a hunting ground for king-fishers, herons, and egrets.

Continue southeast on the path closest to the bluffs. On your left, you'll pass a great wall of exposed yellow sandstone and terra-cotta limestone blocks, as well as another large pond full of fish, birds, and muskrats. At the far end of the pond, you can see the walled-up remains of Wakan Tipi/Carver's Cave, which is the birthplace of the Dakota (more commonly known by the derogatory name the Sioux), according to their creation story. The front part of the cave was destroyed in the 1860s during railroad magnate James J. Hill's various construction projects, as were ancient petroglyphs that filled the entrance of the cave. It was boarded up in the 1970s to prevent further desecration.

Turn around and take the path closest to the train tracks, headed northwest. Continue north-west all the way past the pond. All along the path are hundreds of native wildflowers and plants, including tiny daisylike dogbanes, yellow black-eyed Susans, and giant purple coneflowers.

Go left past the second pond and the floodplain forest restoration area, headed southwest. Go straight past the next fork to walk up close to the train tracks. Some of the oldest and largest trees in the sanctuary are in this area. Follow the path as it curves right, northwest.

At the next fork in the path, turn right. Turn left at the next fork and go straight. Exit the sanctuary and go straight through the parking lot. Cross Commercial Street to return to the walking path, and follow the path uphill. At the stop sign at the top of the hill, make a right into ❷ **Indian Mounds Regional Park**. Follow the path to the overlook and back to Mounds Boulevard. Take a right on Mounds Boulevard.

At the next fork take a right to walk alongside the scenic overlook. Below and to the right are more great views of St. Paul and the Mississippi River, as well as Holman Field, a small airstrip from which small private and military planes regularly take off. Down on the river, gigantic freight barges pass by with their loads, much as they've done since the 19th century.

Stay right all the way up the hill and toward the beacon on its highest point. Just before you reach the beacon, take a right and an immediate left to continue up the steep hill. This takes you alongside the "airway" beacon for Holman Field. The beacon was built in 1929 to assist airmail delivery for the U.S. Postal Service planes leaving Holman Field.

Go straight on the path to see the Indian Mounds, the park's namesake. Until the early 1980s, you could walk around on these mounds. To protect them from further damage, the iron gates were erected. The mounds were once much larger, but they were leveled during ill-conceived construction and landscaping projects in the late 19th century.

Turn right at the second mound to follow the retaining wall. Follow the path past the third and fourth mounds, and then go straight to see the fifth and sixth mounds. After the sixth mound, turn left and continue around to your left. On your left is a big picnic pavilion, located at Mounds Boulevard and Earl Street, which is a great spot for eating your bag lunch.

Go straight downhill on the combined bicycle/pedestrian path. In front of the beacon is a plaque about the structure, the last of its kind. On a clear day, you can see both downtown St. Paul and the Minneapolis skyline from here—look for the Minneapolis skyscrapers nestled between the Cathedral of Saint Paul and the state capitol.

Go all the way down the hill to the park entrance and parking lot where you started.

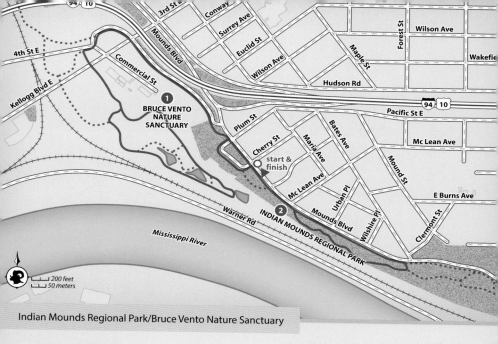

Indian Mounds Regional Park/Bruce Vento Nature Sanctuary

Points of Interest

1 **Bruce Vento Nature Sanctuary** nps.gov/miss/planyourvisit/ventosanctuary.htm, 4th St. East and Commercial St., St. Paul, 651-266-6400

2 **Indian Mounds Regional Park** stpaul.gov/facilities/indian-mounds-regional-park, 10 Mounds Blvd., St. Paul, 651-632-5111

35 Payne-Phalen
Picnic in the Park, Southeast Asian–Style

Above: Pathway around Lake Phalen

BOUNDARIES: E. Ames Ave., Wheelock Pkwy., Phalen Dr., Frost Ave., E. Shore Dr.
HUDSON'S TWIN CITIES STREET ATLAS COORDINATES: Map 396, 3B and 4B
DISTANCE: About 3.75 miles
DIFFICULTY: Moderate
PARKING: Free parking in the lot at beginning of walk
PUBLIC TRANSIT: Bus lines 61 and 64

Over the years the ethnic dynamic of Payne-Phalen has changed, but Lake Phalen remains at its center. Located at the northern corner of the neighborhood and St. Paul (a portion extends into suburban Maplewood), the lake—the city's original water supply—was acquired in 1899. The 278-acre public park opened in time for the first wave of predominantly Swedish immigration, and each successive generation has enjoyed the swimming beach and picnicked in the park. The east-side neighborhood has remained solidly blue-collar as Italians, Latinos, and, most recently, Mexicans and the Hmong from Southeast Asia have arrived. The ethnic minority from Laos fought against the communist Pathet Lao during the Vietnam War. In 1975 the federal government recognized their service, and over four decades 250,000 Hmong moved to the United States. Today, Minnesota trails only California in total number of Hmong residents.

The annual Dragon Festival in July celebrates the area's wealth of pan-Asian culture. The two-day event includes food, music, arts, martial arts, and the dragon boat race. Based on a competition originating in China more than 2,400 years ago, teams of 20 compete in colorful 40-by-4-foot boats rowing to a drumbeat as thousands of multigenerational spectators relax on the shores of Lake Phalen.

Walk Description

Start at the northwesternmost parking lot of ❶ **Phalen Park**, and follow the innermost walking path down the hill and over the bridge. Cross the bridge over the creek connecting Round Lake and Lake Phalen. On your left is *Meditation* by world-famous sculptor Lei Yixin of Changshu, China, a St. Paul sister city. Over the years he has created hundreds of public sculptures, ranging from Mao Zedong in China to the Martin Luther King Jr. National Memorial in Washington, D.C.

Go under the bridge, keep left, and merge with the bike path, passing the playground and picnic pavilion. Follow the path immediately right after passing the memorial statue of the Civilian Conservation Corps, and stay in the pedestrian lane ascending the hill.

Continue on the wending path, passing ❷ **Phalen Park Golf Course** on the right across the street. Follow the pedestrian path around the Lake Phalen Beach House. Then continue on the walking path closest to the lake at the beach house—the only lakeside public swimming beach in St. Paul. The path again merges with the bike lane, passing the watershed district's abundance of cattails and bird nests as it curves around the lake.

Turn right, following the pedestrian path and walking away from the lake to the intersection of East Shore Drive and Wheelock Parkway/Johnson Parkway. Then cross East Shore on Johnson Parkway. Originally platted in Suburban Hills near the Mounds Park neighborhood, the street, it is speculated, was named in honor of surveyor Gates Johnson. In 1930 the street was extended into a parkway terminating at Lake Phalen and was rededicated in honor of John A. Johnson, who served as Minnesota governor from 1905 to 1909. Of Swedish descent, he was the first Minnesota-born governor. At the 1908 Democratic Convention, he was nominated for president but lost to William Jennings Bryan. Tragically, he was the state's first governor to die in office.

Stop at the Hmong Village food courts for a taste of Southeast Asia.

After crossing Phalen Boulevard, on the left is Phalen Crossing, the heart of the city's Phalen Corridor revitalization, completed in 2004: 300 units of condos and townhomes stretched over 14 acres. A restored pond and roads replaced the site of a dilapidated east-side shopping mall.

Turn right, crossing Johnson Parkway, and turn left immediately, following the sidewalk. Continue a quarter mile. On the right is ❸ **Hmong Village**, a triumph of the American immigrant mom-and-pop business. The nondescript exterior of the former warehouse building belies what's inside: more than 230 merchant stalls with traditional Hmong clothing, CDs, DVDs, jewelry, groceries, a farmers market, and, of course, food—delicious food that will stuff a family of four for less than $25. The flavors of Southeast Asia: pho, *chow fun,* egg rolls, spring rolls, Hmong sausage, papaya salad, and so much more provide a yummy escape, regardless of the weather outside.

When your visit to Hmong Village is over, turn around, turning left on Johnson Parkway, and follow the path back to Phalen Boulevard. Turn right and then left on Johnson Parkway. Cross East Shore Drive and turn left, following the lake to the beach house. Follow the path right, crossing the parking lot along the lake. Descending the hill, follow the middle path, passing the playground again and native wildflowers on the right as the path veers under the bridge.

After crossing the bridge, on the left across the creek and up the hill is the Ice Palace Plaque. The plaque commemorates the centennial of the St. Paul Winter Carnival in 1986; the ice structure included towers as high as 128 feet, and for the short time before it melted, it attracted more than a million visitors.

Cross the next bridge and walk to the parking lot, our starting point.

Points of Interest

1 **Phalen Park** stpaul.gov/facilities/phalen-regional-park, 1600 Phalen Dr., St. Paul, 651-632-5111

2 **Phalen Park Golf Course** stpaul.golf/phalen-park-gc, 1615 Phalen Dr., St. Paul, 651-778-0413

3 **Hmong Village** 1001 Johnson Pkwy., St. Paul, 651-777-7886

Appendix: Walks by Theme

Natural Spaces

Lake Calhoun/Bde Maka Ska (Walk 2)
Lake Harriet (Walk 3)
Loring Park and the Walker Art Center (Walk 7)
Bridge Square, the Gateway, Boom Island, Nicollet Island, and the North Loop (Walk 12)
Minnehaha Parkway/48th and Chicago (Walk 22)
Minnehaha Falls (Walk 23)
Highland Park and Hidden Falls Regional Park (Walk 24)
High Bridge and Cherokee Regional Park (Walk 26)
Como Park (Walk 29)
Swede Hollow/Dayton's Bluff (Walk 33)
Indian Mounds Regional Park/Bruce Vento Nature Sanctuary (Walk 34)
Payne-Phalen (Walk 35)

Historic Areas

Phillips and Elliot Park (Walk 6)
Minneapolis Downtown and Theater District (Walk 9)
Downtown/Washington Avenue (Walk 10)
Warehouse District/North Loop (Walk 11)
Bridge Square, the Gateway, Boom Island, Nicollet Island, and the North Loop (Walk 12)
Historic Mill District (Walk 13)
East Hennepin/Marcy-Holmes (Walk 14)
U of M (Walk 17)
Nordeast Minneapolis (Walk 18)
Prospect Park's Tower Hill Park and Water Tower (Walk 20)
Minneapolis's Lake Street (Walk 21)
Minnehaha Falls (Walk 23)
Cathedral, Ramsey, and Summit Hills (Walk 27)
Minnesota State Capitol (Walk 28)
Downtown St. Paul (Walk 31)
Swede Hollow/Dayton's Bluff (Walk 33)
Indian Mounds Regional Park/Bruce Vento Nature Sanctuary (Walk 34)

Dining, Shopping, and Entertainment

Uptown (Walk 1)
Nicollet Avenue's Eat Street (Walk 4)
Cedar-Riverside (Walk 8)
Minneapolis Downtown and Theater District (Walk 9)
Downtown/Washington Avenue (Walk 10)

East Hennepin/Marcy-Holmes (Walk 14)
Dinkytown (Walk 15)
Nordeast Minneapolis (Walk 18)
Minneapolis's Lake Street (Walk 21)
Minnehaha Parkway/48th and Chicago (Walk 22)
Highland Park and Hidden Falls Regional Park (Walk 24)
Cathedral, Ramsey, and Summit Hills (Walk 27)
Irvine Park and West 7th Street (Walk 30)
Downtown St. Paul (Walk 31)
West Side (Walk 32)
Swede Hollow/Dayton's Bluff (Walk 33)
Payne-Phalen (Walk 35)

Around Campus

Dinkytown (Walk 15)
U of M (Walk 17)

Architecture

Whittier (Walk 5)
Phillips and Elliot Park (Walk 6)
Loring Park and the Walker Art Center (Walk 7)
Minneapolis Downtown and Theater District (Walk 9)
Downtown/Washington Avenue (Walk 10)
Warehouse District/North Loop (Walk 11)
Historic Mill District (Walk 13)
U of M (Walk 17)
Nordeast Minneapolis (Walk 18)
Minnesota State Capitol (Walk 28)
Como Park (Walk 29)
Irvine Park and West 7th Street (Walk 30)
Downtown St. Paul (Walk 31)

Index

Able Seedhouse & Brewery, 85
Acadia Café, 37
Afro Deli, 74
Agra Culture Coffee Shop and Café (Mia), 21
Aki's BreadHaus, 86
Alexander Ramsey House, 138, 140
Alfred F. Pillsbury House, 20
Alliance Française, 54
Al's Breakfast, 68
American Swedish Institute (ASI), 24–27
Annie's Parlour restaurant, 67
architecture, best walks for, 165
Ard Godfrey House, 64
Argento, Darlo, 54
Armstrong-Quinlan House, 138
Askov Finlayson, 54
Aster Cafe, 60
Aveda Day Spa Institute, 64

Bachelor Farmer restaurant, 54
Bad Waitress diner, 63
Bad Weather Brewing Company, 117, 118
Baker's Field Flour and Bread Co., 79
Bakken: A Library and Museum of Electricity in
    Life, 7–8
Band Box Diner, 26
Barbette restaurant, 4
Bark and the Bite barbecue joint, 80
Barrio Mexican restaurant, 145
Barthel, Bernard, 113
Basilica of Saint Mary, 31
Bassett, Joel, 53
Bauhaus Brew Labs, 86
Bde Maka Ska/Lake Calhoun, 6–9
Beard's Plaisance Park, 11
Beer Hall and Restaurant, 89–90
Bell, Fames Ford, 24
Beltrami, Giacomo, 84
Beltrami Park, 84

Berryman, John, 75
Betty Danger's Country Club, 79
Big Back Yard, the, 139
Birk, Matt, 110
Bishop, Harriet, 10
Black Forest Inn, 17
Black Sheep pizzeria, 49
Boca Chica Restaurante Mexicano & Cantina, 149
Bohemian Flats Park, 75
Bookmen Loft Condo building, 48
Boom Island, 51–55
Boom Island Park, 52
Botero, Fernando, 44
Bottling House, 82
Boyd, Frank, 124
Boyd Park, 124
Brasa Rotisserie, 63
Brave New Workshop, 40
Bread & Pickle, 13
Brewer's Cave, 156
Brian Coyle Community Center, 35
Bridge Square, the Gateway, Boom Island,
    Nicollet Island, and the North Loop, 51–55
Broders' Cucina Italiana, 11
Broder's Pasta Bar, 11
Brooks, Anson and Georgia, 24
Bruce Vento Nature Sanctuary/Indian Mounds
    Park, 155–159
Bruggen, Coosje van, 32
Bryant Lake Bowl & Cabaret Theater, 63
Buffington, LeRoy, 75
Burger, Warren E., 122

Café Barbette, 63
Café Finspång Scandinavian foods and gifts, 95
Café Lurcat, 31
Cafesjian's Carousel, 132, 134
Calhoun Square, 2, 4
Camden Bridge, 71
Camdi Restaurant, 68
campus, best walks around, 165

Candyland, 144
Cappelen, Frederick, 89
Carlyle Condos, 44
Cass Gilbert works, 121
Cataract Temple, 64
Cathedral, Ramsey, and Summit Hills, 120–125
Cathedral of Saint Paul, 121, 124
Cedar Boulevard, 37
Cedar Cultural Center, 37
Cedar-Riverside, 34–38
Center for Lost Objects, 114
Central Avenue Business District and Northeast
      Breweries Tour, 84–87
Chain of Lakes system, 6
Charles Symonds House, 138
Cheng Heng Restaurant, 130
Cherokee Regional Park and High Bridge,
      116–119
Children's Hospitals and Clinics, 27
Children's Theatre Company, 20
Church of the Assumption, 144
Chute Square, 64
Cleveland, Horace W. S., 100
Cleveland Wok, 108
Clockwerks Brewing, 41
Cloud Man's Village, 6
Community Peace Gardens, 37
Como Golf Course and Cross Country
      Ski Area, 132
Como-Harriet Streetcar Line, 11, 13
Como Lake, 131, 132–133
Como Lakeside Pavilion, 132
Como Park, 131–135
Como Park Zoo & Conservatory, 132
Como Streetcar Station, 134
Corner Coffee, 48
Cossetta Alimentari, 139
Costa Blanca Bistro, 86
Cowles Center for Dance and the
      Performing Arts, 41
Coyle, Brian, 35

Cray Plaza, 143
Currie Park, 35

Dakota Conflict of 1862, 140
Dangerous Man Brewing Co., 81
Dayton's Bluff/Swede Hollow, 151–154
DeLeSalle High School, 54
dining, best walks for, 164–165
Dinkytown, 66–69
District del Sol, 148
Downtown St. Paul, 142–146
Downtown/Washington Avenue, 43–46
Dr. Justus Ohage House, 138
Draft Horse restaurant and charcuterie, 79
Drink, The, 114
Dunn Brothers Coffee, 44
Dylan, Bob, 67, 68

East Hennepin/Marcy-Holmes, 62–65
Eastside restaurant, 44
Eat My Words bookstore, 81
Eat Street, 15–18
Ebenezer Church, 24
Eco-Yard Midtown, 93
Eddy Hall, U of M, 75
Edgewater Park, 79
88 Oriental Foods, 130
El Burrito Mercado, 149
Elliot Park and Phillips, 23–28
El Taco Riendo, 86
English Language Immersion School, 16
entertainment, best walks for, 164–165
Esker Grove, 31

Fair State Brewing Cooperative, 86
Father Hennepin Bluff Park, 57
First Avenue nightclub, 40
First Baptist Church, 40
First Bridge Park, 59
First National Bank Building, 143
Fitzgerald, F. Scott, 121

Fitzgerald Theater, 144
Food Building, 79
Football Pizza, 86
Ford Dam, 104, 109
Ford Motor Company production plant
    (demolished), 108
Ford Road, 112
Ford Twin Cities Assembly Plant, 107
Forepaugh, Joseph, 137
Forepaugh's Restaurant, 137
Fountain Cave, 113
48th and Chicago/Minnehaha Parkway,
    97–101
4 Bells seafood restaurant, 32
Franklin Steele Square, 26
Franklin-Nicollet Liquor, 16
Free Spirit Publishing, 49
Freeport West Inc., 24, 26
Freewheel Bike, 93
Frogtown neighborhood, 128
Fulton Brewery Tap Room, 48

Galtier, Father Lucien, 143
Gardens of Salonica Greek restaurant, 63
Gasthol Zur Gemütlichkeit, 80
Gateway District, 53
Gateway, the, 51–55
Gay 90's, 41
Gehry, Frank, 74
George Latimer Central Library, 145
George Peavey House, 24
George Washington Memorial Flagstaff, 54
Gilbert, Cass, 75
Glam Doll Donuts, 63
Gluek Park, 79
Gluek's Restaurant & Bar, 40
Goat Coffeehouse, 153
Godfrey, Ard and Harriet, 64
Gold Medal Park, 58
Goodfellow, William, 8
Grain Belt Bottling House, 82

Grain Belt Brewery (former), 82
Grand Rounds Scenic Byway, 6, 100
Graves, Michael, 20
Grumpy's bar and restaurant, 45
Guthrie Theater, 44, 58

Half Price Books, 108
Hamm Park, 153
Hamm, Theodore and Louisa, 153
Hamm's Brewery fortress, 152
Happy Gnome, The, 123
Hard Times Cafe, 36
Harvester Lofts, 49
Hennepin Avenue United Methodist Church, 30
Hennepin, George and Leonota, 20
Hennepin History Museum, 20
Hennepin, Louis, 57
Hewitt, Edwin, 30
Hidden Falls Regional Park and Highland
    Park, 107–111
Hidden Falls Regional Park, 110
High Bridge and Cherokee Regional
    Park, 116–119
Highland Café & Bakery, 108
Highland Grill, 108
Highland 1 & 2 theater, 108, 109
Highland Park and Hidden Falls Regional
    Park, 107–111
Highland Village Center, 108
Hill District, 120–125
Hill, James J., 117, 122, 157
Himalayan Restaurant, 67
historic areas, best walks for, 164
Historic Mill District, 56–61
Hmong people, 161
Hmong Village, 162
Holman Field, 158
Holy Cross Catholic Church, 80
Holy Land foods, 86
Hopewell mounds, 155
Hubert H. Humphrey Metrodome, 76

Humphrey, Hubert, 74
Humphrey-Willis House, 138

I Like You shop, 63
Icehouse restaurant, 16
Ice Palace Plaque, 162
Indeed Brewing Company, 85
Indian Mounds Regional Park, 158
Indian Mounds Regional Park/Bruce Vento
    Nature Sanctuary, 155–159
Ingebrefsen's Scandinavian Gifts, 94
Institute for Agricultural and Trade Policy, 21
International Harvester Company of America
    building, 49
In the Heart of the Beast Puppet and Mask
    Theatre, 95
Irene Hixon Whitney Bridge, 29, 30, 31
Irvine Park, 137
Irvine Park and West Seventh Street,
    136–141
Isabel Apartments, 148
Izzy's Ice Cream, 58

Jacob Schmidt Brewing, 113
James, Jessie, 133
James J. Hill Center, 145
James J. Hill House, 124
James J. Hill Reference Library, 122
Jax Cafe, 80
Jay and Henry Knox House, 137
Jefe restaurant, 60
John H. Stevens House, 103
John McDonald House, 138
Johnson, John A., 161
Jones, Robert "Fish," 105
JUN restaurant, 49

Kafé 421, 68
Karpis-Barker gang, 113
Keg and Case marketplace, 114
Kellogg, Frank B., 127–128

Kitty Cat Klub, 67
Kozlak-Radulovich Funeral Chapel, 80
Kramarczuk's deli and restaurant, 64

La Colonia Restaurant, 86
Lagoon Cinema, 3
Lake Calhoun, 3, 7
Lake Calhoun North Beach, 7
Lake Calhoun/Bde Maka Ska, 6–9
Lake Harriet, 10–14
Lake Harriet Band Shell, 13
Lake Harriet Southeast Beach, 12
Lake Nokomis, 95
Lake Nokomis Beach, 98
Lake Phalen, 160
Lakewood Memorial Cemetery, 8, 13
Landmark Center, 144
La Loma, 95
La Loma Tamales, 143
Larrabee, Edward Barnes, 30
Late Night with David Letterman, 142
Layman, Martin, 93
Leavenworth, Colonel Henry, 10
Lemna Technologies, 24
Lerner Publishing Group, 49
Liffey Irish Pub, 139
Little Szechuan Chinese Restaurant
    and Bar, 130
Lock & Dam No. 1, 104, 109
Longfellow Gardens, 105
Longfellow, Henry Wadsworth, 102, 105
Longfellow House, 105
Loring Bar & Restaurant, 67
Loring, Charles, 30
Loring Park, 16, 30, 31
Loring Park and Walker Art Center, 29–33
Loring Park Community Center, 32
Los Ocampo Mexican restaurant, 95
Lovejoy, Harriet, 10
Lumber Exchange Building, 41
Lyndale Park Peace Garden, 11, 12

Lyndale Park Perennial and Annual
    Display Garden, 12
Lyndale Park Rose Garden, 12

MacPhail Center for Music, 45
Mañana Restaurante y Pupuseria, 153
Mankato Kasota Stone building, 59
Manny's Tortas, 95
Marcy-Holmes/East Hennepin, 62–65
Marie Schmidt-Bremer Home, 113
Mario's Keller Bar, 80
Marjorie McNeely Conservatory, 132
Market House by D'Amico, 127
Marshall, William, 137
Masqueray, Emmanuel, 124
Mauer, Joe, 110
Maya Cuisine, 85
Mayday Books, 36
McNamara Alumni Center, 74
McRae Park, 95
Mears Park, 143
Memorial Cemetery, 11
Menchie's frozen yogurt, 108
Mercado Central, 92
Merriam Street Bridge, 60
Mesa Pizza, 4
Metrodome, 43
Mickey's Dining Car, 144
Midtown Global Market, 95
Midtown Greenway, 3, 17, 93, 95
Midwest Mountaineering, 36
Mill City Farmers Market, 59
Mill City Museum, 44, 59
Mill District, Historic, 56–61
Mill Ruins Park, 57
Milwaukee Road Depot, 44
Minneapolis, 1
Minneapolis Armory, 45
Minneapolis College of Art and Design , 20
Minneapolis Downtown and Theater
    District, 39–42

Minneapolis Institute of Arts (Mia), 20, 21
Minneapolis Pioneers and Soldiers Memorial
    Cemetery, 93–94
Minneapolis Sculpture Garden, 30, 32
Minneapolis's Lake Street, 92–96
Minnehaha Depot, 105
Minnehaha Falls, 102–106, 103
Minnehaha Parkway/48th and Chicago, 97–101
Minnehaha Regional Park, 102
Minnesota Children's Museum, 144
Minnesota Governor's Residence, 122
Minnesota History Center, 127
Minnesota State Capitol, 126–130, 127
Minnesota Vietnam Veterans Memorial, 129
Minnesota Zen Meditation Center, 8
Mississippi Market, 122
Mississippi National River and Recreation
    Center, 139
Mississippi River, 1, 51, 52, 53, 56, 57, 70, 75, 79,
    95, 107, 116, 117, 122, 139, 147, 158
Mitchell Hamline School of Law, 122
Mixed Blood Theatre, 36
Modist Brewing Co., 48
Mojsilov, Zoran, 63
Morelli's Italian deli and liquor store, 151
Morris, Jack, 110
Moscow on the Hill restaurant, 123–124
Mounds Park, 161
Murray-Lanpher House, 137

natural spaces, best walks for, 164
New Traditional–style Uptown City
    Apartments, 3
Ngon Vietnamese Bistro, 130
Nicollet Avenue's Eat Street, 15–18
Nicollet Island, 51–55
Nicollet Island Inn, 60
Nicollet Island Park, 54
Nokomis Community Center, 99
Nordeast Minneapolis, 78–83

Northeast Breweries Tour and Central Avenue
  Business District, 84–87
North Loop, 51–55
North Loop Dog Grounds, 48
North Loop/Warehouse District, 47–50
North Mississippi Regional Park, 70
North Mississippi Regional Park and
  Webber Park, 70–72
Nouvel, Jean, 58
Nye's Polonaise Room, 64

Oldenburg, Claes, 32
Old Main, U of M, 76
Olson, Floyd B., 127
Olson, Sara Jane, 108
One on One Bicycle Studio, 49
Open Book building, 45
Ordway Center for the Performing Arts, 145
Orpheum Theatre, 40
Our Lady of Lourdes Catholic Church, 64
Our Lady of Mount Carmel Catholic Church, 85

Palace Theatre, 143–144
Panaderia El Mexicano, 95
Pancho Villa Mexican Restaurant, 17
Pantages Theatre, 40
Parker-Marshall House, 137
Parkway Theater, 100
Parque de Castillo, 149
Parrant, Pierre "Pig's Eye," 113
Patrick McGovern's Pub & Restaurant, 140
Paul and Sheila Wellstone Center for
  Community, 149
Payne-Phalen, 160–163
Peavey Field Park, 27
Peninsula Malaysian Cuisine, 16
Pepito's Mexican restaurant, 100
Phalen Park, 161
Phalen Park Golf Course, 161
Phelan, Edward, 153
Phelps Fountain, 12

Phillips and Elliot Park, 23–28
Pho Tau Bay Vietnamese restaurant, 17
Pierre Bottineau Library, 82
Pillsbury A Mill, 60
Pillsbury, John and Alfred, 21
Pitts, Charlie, 132
Pizza Lucé, 49
Plymouth Congregational Church, 16
Pracna restaurant and bar, 60
Pratt Community School, 89
Prospect Park's Tower Hill Park and Water
  Tower, 88–91
Psycho Suzi's Motor Lounge, 79
Pumphouse Creamery, 98, 100
Punch Neopolitan Pizza, 64
Purple Onion Café, 67

Quadriga horse sculptures, 127
Quang Vietnamese restaurant, 17

Rainbow Chinese Restaurant and Bar, 17
Ramsey, Alexander, 140
Ramsey, Cathedral, and Summit Hills, 120–125
Rappahannock apartments, 26
Rapson, Ralph, 35, 68
Red Cow burgers, 123
Red Rabbit Italian cuisine, 49
Red Stag Supperclub, 63
Red Table Meat Co., 79
Reid, Tom, 140
Revival restaurant, 122
Rice Park, 143, 144
Riggs, Dudley, 40
Ritz Theater, 81
Riverplace, 60
Riverside, 34–38
Riverside Plaza, 35
Roat Osha Thai restaurant, 4
Roberts, Alex, 63
Roberts Bird Sanctuary, 11, 12
Roberts, Thomas Sadler, 12

Rogue Buddha Gallery, 81
Roman Catholic Archdiocese of St. Paul and
    Minneapolis, 1

Sabo, Martin Olav, 93
Saint Sabrina's, 3
Saint Thomas More Catholic Community, 122
Saloon, The, 40
Salty Tart, 95
Sample Room restaurant, 79
Sandcastle restaurant, 98
Schmidt Artist Lofts, 114
Schmidt Brewing Company, 113
Schmidt, Jacob, Marie, and Edward, 113
Schulz, Charles, 139
Science Museum of Minnesota, 139
Sea Salt Eatery, 103
Sen Yai Sen Lek Thai food, 86
Seventh Street Improvement Arches, 151
Sex World, 49
Shamrocks: The Irish Nook, 114
shopping, best walks for, 164–165
Simpson-Wood House, 137
Smack Shack lobster restaurant, 49
"Snoose Boulevard," 37
Somali Education Center, 16
Soo Line Bridge, 71
Southeast Asian cuisine, 129
Southeast Community Library, 68
Spoon and Stable restaurant, 54
Spoonbridge and Cherry public art, 31, 32
Spoonriver restaurant, 59
Spring Café, 132
Spyhouse Coffee Company, 85
Spyhouse Expresso Bar and Gallery, 16
SS. Cyril & Methodius Catholic Church, 81
Stahlmann Cave Brewery, 113
St. Anthony, 57
St. Anthony Falls, 57, 60
St. Anthony Main Theatre, 60
State Capital Credit Union, 68

State Theatre, 41
Steele, Franklin, 57
Stella's Fish Café & Prestige Oyster Bar, 4
Stevens, Colonel John, 53
St. Mark's Episcopal Cathedral, 30
St. Mary's Greek Orthodox Church, 8
St. Mary's University campus, 24
St. Michael's Catholic Church, 148
Stone Arch Bridge, 57
Straitgate Church, 26
St. Paul, 1
St. Paul's Downtown, 142–146
St. Paul's Evangelical Cathedral, 30
St. Paul's Evangelical Lutheran Church, 26
St. Paul's Flat Earth brewery, 153
Stub & Herb's bar and restaurant, 76
Summit, Cathedral, and Ramsey Hills, 120–125
Summit Overlook Park, 121
Sumner and Eugenie McKnight House, 26
Supatra's Thai Cuisine, 114
Surly Bill, 1
Surly Brewing Co., 89
Svenska Dalen, 151
Swede Hollow Cafe, 153
Swede Hollow/Dayton's Bluff, 151–154
Swede Hollow Park, 151
Symbionese Liberation Army, 108

Taqueria Los Paisanos, 153
Target Field, 48
Tattersall Distilling's cocktail lounge, 85
Taylor, President Zachary, 140
TeaSource, 108
Ten Thousand Villages, 122–123
Terzo wine bar, 11
Theater District and Minneapolis
    Downtown, 39–42
Theater Latté Da, 81
32nd Street Beach, 8
Thomas Beach, 8
Thomas Sadler Roberts Bird Sanctuary, 13

Thompson, T. Eugene, 108
Thune, Dave, 113
Tibet Arts & Gifts, 95
Tibet Store, 3
Tom Reid's Hockey City Pub, 140
Torre de San Miguel Homes, 148–149
Totino's Pizza, 63
Tower Hill observation deck, 90
Tower Hill Park, 89
Town Hall Tap, 100
TractorWorks Building, 48
Turnblad, Swan J., 24, 27
Turtle Bread Company, 100
Twin/Tone Records, 17
Uncle Edgar's Mystery Bookstore, 93
Uncle Hugo's Science Fiction Bookstore, 93
University of Minnesota (U of M), 34, 35, 36,
    66, 73–77
Upper St. Anthony Falls Lock and Dam, 57
Uptown, 2–5
Uptown Art Fair, 4
Uptown Theatre, 3
U.S. Bank Stadium, 43, 45

Varsity Theater, 68
Veterans Service Building, 128
Virginia Street Church, 124
Vrancic, Faust, 93

Wabasha Brewing Company, 149
Wabasha Street Bridge, 147
W. A. Frost & Company, 123
Wagner-Marty House, 137
Wakan Tipi/Carver's Cave, 157
Waldmann Brewery & Wurstery, 117, 118
Walker Art Center and Loring Park, 29–33
Walker Sculpture Garden, 31
Walker, Thomas, 30
walks. See also specific walk
    categorized by theme, 164–165
Wally's restaurant, 68

Warehouse District/North Loop, 47–50
Warren E. Burger Library, 122
Washburn A Mill Complex, 58
Washburn Fair Oaks Park, 20, 21
Washburn, William, 20
Washington Avenue/Downtown, 43–46
Water Power Park, 60
Water Tower, Prospect Park, 89
Webber, Charles C. and Mary, 71
Webber Park and North Mississippi Regional
    Park, 70–72
Webber Park and swimming pool, 71
Weisman Art Museum, 74
West Seventh Street, 112–115
West Seventh Street and Irvine Park,
    136–141
West High School, 3
West Side, 147–150
Whitney, William Channing, 21
Whittier, 15, 19–22
Wienery, 37
Wilde Roast Café, 60
Wilkins, Roy, 127
Williams Arena, U of M, 76
Williams Uptown Pub & Peanut Bar, 3
Wirth, Theodore, 12
Woman's Club of Minneapolis, 32
Wright-Pendergast House, 138

Xcel Energy Center, 137, 139

Yarusso-Bros. Italian Restaurant, 151
Yixin, Lei, 161
Yoerg Saloon, 149
Young Joni restaurant, 82

Zen Box Izakaya restaurant, 44
Zimmerman, Robert, 67, 68
Zuhrah Shrine Temple, 24

About the Authors

photographed by Wolfgang Wick

photographed by Astrid Wick

Holly Day's writing has appeared in more than 3,500 publications internationally, including *Computer Music Journal, ROCKRGRL, Music Alive!, Guitar One, Brutarian Magazine, Interface Technology,* and *Mixdown Magazine.* Over the past couple of decades, she has received an Isaac Asimov Award, a National Magazine Award, and two Midwest Writer's Grants for her work. Her books include *The Insider's Guide to the Twin Cities* and *Music Theory for Dummies.*

Sherman Wick is a native of the Twin Cities. Since receiving a history degree at the University of Minnesota, he has worked as a freelance writer and photographer, focusing on music, film, and Minnesota's rich cultural and historical offerings.

Holly and Sherman started writing their first book together, *The Insider's Guide to the Twin Cities,* one week after marrying and have since written *Nordeast Minneapolis: A History, A Brief History of Stillwater Minnesota* and the forthcoming *History Lovers' Guide to Minneapolis.* They live near downtown Minneapolis with their daughter, Astrid.